TO SEA

As a little girl at sc... stories were written w... my sons were small, I s... made up exciting bed time adventures. I wrote many varied articles, letters and personal stories which were published in women's magazines such as Chat, Woman's Own, Woman, Take a break, My Weekly, Bella and local newspapers. Many years ago I had a makeover, courtesy of The Daily Mail in the Femail section and a full page spread and thought wow is that me?

I have appeared on over sixty TV programmes, films and magazine shoots. I spent hours cutting up and gouging out a real coconut to make a tropical themed bra, so I could sing, 'I've got a lovely bunch of coconuts,' at the X Factor auditions. My Hawaiian outfit impressed the judges but my screeching cleared the room.

When I am not writing, I work as a volunteer at an animal rescue centre walking the dogs. I also work as a volunteer for Marie Curie Cancer care. I embrace swimming, belly dancing, scuba diving, cocktails, champagne, eating and adore my gorgeous sons, husband and love my family to bits.

This is a true story, though some conversations may not be word for word. Additionally, some people's names have been changed to protect their identity.

ALANA COWELL
TO SEA OR NOT TO SEA

Life is more than a crazy journey. I thank my husband for his continuous hard work for his family. He is a wonderful dad. Both of my son's love and presence have showered my life with rainbows and treasure. Every second brings a positive or negative phase from the moment we are put on this earth. Having a sense of humour is the best gift I possess.

Thank you to James Cunningham who worked hard to produce and design the fantastic book cover.

My admiration never ends for the RNLI who risk their lives to search and rescue people who are in trouble at sea, on shore or on the cliffs. A visit to the Solent Coastguard left me blown away. I had no idea how complex and amazing their roles are for our safety and saving lives at sea. Thank you to L and M who encouraged me when I had writer's block. Thank you to Robert for helping us at difficult times. I love you Kacie with all my heart. You are a wonderful sister.

I apologise for some of the naughtiness or clichés in the book but they describe real life experiences. My book is a bit 'off the wall' - you'll either love it or hate it. If you do not have a sense of humour put it down now. If you want a book full of sex put it down now. Are you male or female with lips that have the potential to smile and shoulders that shake when you laugh? If yes, then read on. Chill out and giggle.

Lastly my advice to my mother is, don't have sex on the ironing board again!

4

CONTENTS

THE GREEN EYED MONSTER

I was flying the plane single handed but had never flown before. Full throttle and the plane accelerated...within seconds the ground was falling away beneath us. Suddenly over the radio I heard, 'Emergency, emergency.' The instructor grabbed the headphones and put them on quickly. I could tell there was something seriously wrong as he looked frantically from left to right.

'What's wrong?' I asked.

He explained that another plane was on a crash course heading straight for us. He had overshot the runway and his radio and instruments had failed. Clearance could not be given and it was our responsibility to avoid him. We had to spot it quickly before something drastic happened.

I went a stiff as a board, petrified my eyes darted in all directions trying to see the rogue plane. I could see nothing but clouds. His breathing grew louder. I could feel sweat forming on my face, my heart banged in my chest. I tilted my head and peered under the wing. Screaming at the pilot I could see the plane surging towards us. 'There, there! To my right! It's heading straight at us.' I yelled. The pilot grabbed the controls and took a nose dive, my heart leapt into my mouth. I anxiously vomited everywhere as the plane whizzed just over the top of us. I was a nervous wreck.

When Alex told me he'd booked a flying lesson for my 21st birthday present my legs had turned to jelly. I'd never been in an aircraft before. It had nearly ended in a disaster but I'd enjoyed it immensely. I hankered for those exciting days.

Today twenty nine years on I thought I would burst with frustration. My hands were clenched tightly as I experienced an intense feeling of irritability raging through my body. I could stand it no longer.

'For crying out loud, this is ridiculous.' I could feel my nostrils flaring big time. It crossed my mind that Formula 1 racing might be a little more attractive to look at than my angry face.

Were the wall's closing in on me? An overwhelming sense of claustrophobia ran through me. I wanted to flee from the house. I threw my arms in the air.

'We are wasting our lives away here, you constantly watching that box.' My eyebrows rose with despair. 'You have sat there and watched football, rugby and now you're going to watch the blasted motor racing. I keep waiting around this house for hours, bored out of my brain. I'm like a spare part, thinking, "Are you actually going to bother to spend any time with me today?"'

Standing open mouthed, a few throaty growls, I dropped my arms beside my attention craving body. Seething, I could feel a serious temper tantrum looming. Glaring directly at him, with gritted teeth, I waited for an answer. My blood pressure rocketed through the roof and any patience I had left bubbled away.

Alex stared in my direction for a few seconds, firmly perched on the comfy green leather sofa, his arms hung inside his legs. He looked towards the shaggy carpet. I poked my chin towards him. 'Well?' I said, questioning his intentions.

'It's just I wanted to see this,' he replied, pointing to the television and mimicking a puppy dog with his big brown eyes. Did he expect me to express sorrow at trying to take his precious sport away?

'Right I am not staying here another minute waiting for a bloody miracle,' I bellowed, taking in a big breath to muster up some energy.

Rushing out of the lounge and into the hall, I grappled at the hooks, grabbing the first coat I set my eyes on. 'I am going for a drive.' My heart was racing.

I made a quick exit from the house, slamming the door, just to reinforce the feeling to him that I was utterly and thoroughly pissed off.

Tripping down the step, I wobbled on my heel, falling sideways onto the grass. I suspected that I looked a right tit sprawled out on the dewy ground. Jumping up, I regained my posture. Grass stains ran all the way down the left leg of my white jeans. They were ruined. I huffed. Changing them at this crucial point of drama seemed not to be an option.

I took a sneaky peak behind me to make sure he hadn't seen me fall but all I could see was the back of his hair through the window. Head held high, I had been focused to make my exit intense, to create an impact. Shame it had been with the grass. I knew his arse would still be firmly stuck to the seat.

Once again another sunny weekend spoilt, the demon television ruled. Plonking myself behind the wheel, I revved up the engine. I mulled over how tedious life had become. Foot on the accelerator, I screeched away. Driving off down the road, I was livid. Speeding along the winding country lanes, I tried concentrating at each bend. Various tones of green leaves hung down from thick trunked trees forming a tunnel effect. The sun shone through the spindly branches, glistening occasionally creating a blinding light. I had no idea where I was going but just continued driving, savouring the freedom of the countryside.

Driving through Newick, a tiny quaint village sporting a pub on the green, I felt compelled to stop and be nosy. 'Village Fete Today' said an amateur painted sign, sprawled between two bushes that caught my eye. Pulling over in a tight space between a camper home and commercial van, I decided to venture in to the fete.

Loneliness surged over me yet again, as I swept onto the lush green field. It hurt seeing many couples laughing and holding hands. Crowds of excited people milled about. I looked around the field cringing. I was the only person on my own that I could see.

'Come on, jolly up Alana,' I whispered, encouraging my flagging enthusiasm and quickening my pace through the long grass. Most people appeared to be having fun, except me. I needed a fix to cheer me up.

Licking my lips, I mastered the art of sucking on an Oyster ice cream, squeezing the shell together so the softened ice cream oozed out at the sides. Nibbling on the chocolate covered flakes of coconut brought some inner peace but just for a moment.

'Want to have a go at sausage lobbing lady?' A burly lad of around thirteen years of age waved his sausage at me. Shuffling forward he placed it in my hand. It did not seem I had a choice.

'That's twenty pence to have a go and if you win, you get fifty pounds.' Clutching the stocking tightly, I struggled to give him the money from the change of my ice cream. I lined myself up.

My muscles strained. I leant far back and swung my arm, flinging my sausage as hard as I could. Wallop! It landed between my feet and so did the rest of my ice cream. The spectators laughed. My sausage had travelled zero distance. Oh the embarrassment!

I bent down, picked it up and handed the tights filled with sand back to two giggling teenage girls. They playfully threw it towards the young lad. Humiliated, I started heading straight back to my car, contemplating my next move. I decided to drive to the marina at Brighton and have some lunch.

Seventeen miles away lay my destination so I pointed the car towards the M23. Music blaring to try to cheer me up, I sped towards the sea, singing along to some memorable '70s tunes.

Parking the car, I proceeded to the boardwalk lined with snazzy restaurants and wonderful views. Shiny white yachts which were moored on long wooden pontoons waved in the breeze. Preoccupied with wanting to eat pizza, I could see one vacant table right outside the busy Italian restaurant. Their pizzas are scrummy. Taking a deep breath, I breezed through and took a seat. Perched awkwardly at a table for two, I scanned the menu.

Laughter, chatter and delicious smells filled the air. I kept looking around me but I felt lonely. Lifting my shoulders back, I embraced the soothing sun on my face.

Waiting for ages, a tight lipped waitress appeared in front of me blocking out the rays and poised her pen. Looking at the empty chair opposite me, she stared as much as to say, 'Oh dear, poor thing, she's on her own.' Did I see pity in her eyes as she took my order?

Showing interest in my mobile phone, I spent a good ten minutes texting. 'Shit, they are going to think I have been stood up,' I mumbled.

Cringing inside an uncomfortable aura consumed me. I fidgeted, glanced about and put the phone down onto the table. My eyes resembled two full moons as I saw my glass of wine being brought to the table. 'Serious comfort at last', I sighed.

Placing the wine down on the table the waitress's tight lips softened when she smiled. As she turned away on her tiny court heel, I knocked the glass of wine over, smashing the delicate rim. It splattered wine all up the back of the waitress's trim legs. 'What the...' She shrieked wildly, whizzing round towards me. I'd grabbed the stem of

11

the glass a little too late. Diners rubbernecked, showing more interest in my unfortunate accident than their meals.

'Blimey, I am so sorry. I don't know what happened. It just went over,' I prattled on, lying. It was nothing to do with the fact I had clumsily under-estimated my own finger length due to my newly applied false gel nails! Stifled giggles sounded out from other customers as the waitress bustled around trying to clear up the mess and wipe her legs down. How many times today was I going to be overwhelmed with wanting the ground to open up and swallow me?

Placing another glass of Sauvignon Blanc on the table, I continued to endure the sullen looks of the wine soaked waitress. Sheepishly I munched on my pizza and salad, and sipped my wine; I finally relaxed as the alcohol took effect. I enjoyed my food but felt quite awkward. I decided to go for a walk.

Moving through the busy tables, I nodded and waved goodbye to the waitress. I'd left her a decent tip - she deserved that much. This lunch did not turn out how I had imagined it, in fact the whole day had been utterly shit.

Sauntering along the path, I noticed some yachts in the distance. Eagerly I stepped up my pace towards them. They were definitely calling my name.

'Come and admire me Alana, feast your eyes on my erect mast, savour my sleek sail.' Yeah right, of course they were.

Turning a slight corner, a tidy line of tethered yachts caught my interest but one in particular captured my eye. Sat at the back behind the wheel in the cockpit were a man and woman. I seethed as the green eyed monster reared its ugly head. I slyly watched the couple drinking champagne, huddled together and smiling longingly into each other's gaze.

Oblivious to me glancing in their direction, they just seemed completely engrossed in each other and the attention she was receiving had me reeling.

'Why can't my husband be like that?' I questioned myself. 'Why am I standing here on my own, yet again?'

My posture sank, my ribs caved in, I felt abandoned for yet another weekend. I peered cautiously from the corner of my eye.

Was it the bubbly they were sipping, that made them seem so in love? Had they just met? Were they married? Why wasn't it me sipping the champagne, sitting on that lovely yacht, basking in the sun?

My mind was racing, torpedoed with what ifs? I shifted along a little bit more, holding the steel rail, feeding it through my sweaty hands. Edging towards the canoodling couple, I watched closely, so envious it hurt.

Leaning forward their lips touched. He gently stroked her long hair, tucking the end in around her neck towards her pretty face. Tenderly he swept his hand across her cheek. Within minutes they were eating each other's face off. Their embraces became passionate and I felt uncomfortable to witness their lust.

Attempting to avert my eyes was not successful. I was drawn to their clinches, creatively engrossing myself as if I was watching a movie unfolding before me. But it was I who was making the story up and guessing their quests.

I longed to be that woman, drinking the champagne, being adored, in no doubt feeling I was special. He took her hand and led her down into the hull. 'Oh my word, you lucky devil. Humpy bumpy is on the cards for you,' I hissed under my breath. I imagined the steam coming off them. My life felt so shitty at that moment, so lonely. I'd have to go home later but maybe I should consider staying away for a few days.

I leant on the safety rail for another five minutes or so, just taking in the sights. My eyes were focusing on the back of the boat when I realised there was a 'For Sale' sign on it. The very boat in which they were probably now testing the cabins! Could I see the yacht rocking? The prominent 'For Sale' sign definitely rocked my boat!

That could be me. I yearned to be sitting there in the future. Had I gone mad? I was trying to convince myself that I could be sitting on that yacht drinking champagne, looking chic and glamorous. How could that be?

I rubbed my forehead. A price tag of £70,000! Hold your head in shame you silly moo. That's not going to happen, never! Thoughts of buying it inspired me. I visualised myself in a bikini, sipping champagne, sunbathing on the deck, perfect, perfect, perfect.

The 'For Sale' sign read Ancasta Boat Sales. My keen eyes darted around the shopping square looking for the shop. There it was, located just behind me. Ancasta's front window seemed to be flashing, drawing me in. 'Come to me, come to me Alana.'

Round and round the thoughts were rushing in and before I knew it I had run over, burst in through the door and pointing my eager finger directly at the yacht, blurted, 'Can I see that boat please?' A tallish, mature, slim man got out of his chair and walked over.

'Sorry, I'm shutting now. Can you come back tomorrow? We are supposed to shut at 4 o'clock today, being a bank holiday Sunday, and it is ten minutes past now,' he said, holding the door open. I expect he thought I was a timewaster but that was fair enough. If I did come up with the cash I'd be back.

'I wanted to see that boat, the one where they were sitting, sipping champagne. It looked so lovely.' My eyes sparkled with excitement as I recalled their embraces.

'No sorry, not today,' he enforced. 'The owner is on board and I really have to go now. Like I said, I should have closed earlier. You can come back tomorrow. We open at 10.00am,' he encouraged.

Nice chap I thought. Maybe barging in on the owner's afternoon romp might be a bit extreme. I wondered what would have happened if the salesman had said yes!

I gazed to the heavens. It's not my day today, is it? I bemused. Experiencing another sense of loss, I thanked the salesman and left.

An unusual slight chill filled the air so I pulled my lightweight jacket tighter around me. I slowly walked away, glancing back many times at the yacht that I had admired.

Climbing the stairs in the multi-storey car park, I managed to avoid being crushed by noisy stampeding children; who were probably on their way to a party at the bowling alley or cinema. Jumping inside the car, I gripped the wheel, a tinge of excitement sweeping through me.

DRUGS ARE NO GLAMOUR

Could this be a way out of this never ending cycle of boredom at home?

For years, Alex has worked in the depths of London in plush offices. His lunches delivered and put in a fridge by his desk; if he isn't out in pubs or wine bars.

I however, had been employed in back breaking, mind blowing crisis settings. Originally I had worked for a year as a volunteer whilst studying to be a crisis/addiction counsellor. I enjoyed the challenging role of support worker in a detox day centre for people with substance misuse, primarily heroin, cocaine and alcohol. Then I progressed on to university where I took part in a professional development course and gained my diploma in counselling.

In time I secured paid employment with the same company with which I had done my voluntary work. It was gruelling work but I stayed for four years, working in residential care for the first phase of a nine month detox project.

Now my lunch breaks were another matter. I once reluctantly dined on a fine apple crumble made by one of our residential clients. 'Oh please Alana, try my delicious dessert. I picked the apples from the garden especially for us all.' Puddings had never featured much in my life since childhood and agreeing to try the sweet had indeed required a big effort on my part.

We were seated around a large wooden oblong table. Most of us praised Sasha. 'That was superb,' I lied, my gagging reflexes trying to kick in but I'd suppressed them through an unnatural smile. 'Which bowl did you use to mix the crumble in? It must have been pretty large! Did we have one big enough?'

Shuffling my chair forward and leaning slightly on my side, I peered down to the other end of the table, so I could see her.

'I found a sizeable bowl under the stairs,' Sarah said.

'Oh no, you didn't?' I gasped, grabbing the sides of my head. 'We use those for foot detoxes during the relaxation period.'

Terrible retching and heaving noises circled the room. My immediate thought was that we'd experienced a serious breach of health and safety. Would there be trouble?

'Oh dear, that mustn't happen again. We are governed by strict codes of conduct in the kitchen. Everyone has the rules of the kitchen explained to them on arrival.' They all agreed, nodding. To this day I don't understand how I didn't vomit!

My office was cramped. It was about 4ft by 4ft with no windows and a tired little desk. The only thing I had which was useful was an obvious sense of humour.

Firstly, I would assess clients for treatment. It was immensely rewarding to watch a person so addicted to drugs, turn their life around.

One woman arrived on our front doorstep begging for help. I led her through to the back garden. She leaned her tiny emaciated frame against the brick wall. Her hair was dirty and knotted. She needed immediate help as it was clear that it would not be long before she would die. Taking her frail arm, I sat her down on a step and asked a colleague to make some toast and tea. Her lips were so weak she found it difficult to drink from the cup. I pulled off tiny bits of toast and eased them into her mouth.

Her whole being was ravaged by drugs. Her arms and legs were bruised from injecting and she had sunken cheeks and eyes. Her life was ebbing away.

Nine months later, her hair was clean and shining, she had put on a couple of stones in weight and her eyes sparkled. She was beautiful. She was drug free and working tirelessly towards getting her children back in her life. I was so impressed with her hard work.

I was proud that I'd had great success key working with some of my clients and seeing them recapture their quality of life. Unfortunately, looking into a mum's eyes, informing her that her son had just died from an overdose had left dark shadows of the past in my memory too. Whoever thinks there is anything glamorous about taking drugs needs their head testing.

Addiction destroys people and their families. I have seen clients losing major parts of their limbs due to abscesses caused by injecting sites having become infected.

I try to focus on my client's positives and talents. Every one of us is a miracle in our own right. We just need to find out what we are good at.

I will never forget one of my clients, Ben. He showed exceptional talent in his art work and poetry. He was intelligent but lacked self-belief. I worked for many months trying to encourage him to care for his body and appearance. Twisting his hands together nervously, his fingernails were lined with dirt. Throughout his childhood and as a young adult he'd pulled his hair out in chunks. 'Why do you want us to all be the same?' he confronted me, shifting back to sit more upright in the sofa.

'I don't want you all to be the same, I just want you to try to respect who you are, to love and look after yourself and to learn to care about you. Then you will move on.'

Painstakingly, over eight months we did make emotional progress and conquered his compulsion to tear out his hair. It was now thankfully growing but still thin, lank and dirty. I knew that for him to succeed, he needed to accept and nurture himself.

It was my leaving group today. We gathered in the large lounge so that I could say farewell to my inspirational clients and colleagues after four years at the rehab. It was going to be difficult.

Warmly the clients said their goodbyes, placing a big bunch of sunflowers in my lap. Each person spoke to me individually, expressing their feedback on my help, including their progress to date and their ambitions for the future.

Throughout the session I glanced around the room but there was one person missing, Ben. Despite the babble, in the room, I felt a deep quiet sadness. I wondered why he had not come; maybe it was for many reasons.

Week after week, we had worked hard together. I suspected he hated me on some days. On many occasions he'd become defensive. I'd never give in, encouraging him to visualise a different situation to his perceived experiences, psychologically driving him forwards. Maybe he was sad, possibly angry for me leaving too?

Always keeping to strict codes of conduct, hugging was forbidden but the clients didn't seem to care today. One by one they grabbed me to say goodbye, squeezing me tight, thanking me for my kindness and care. Whilst one of the women stood and cried, I took her hand, gently placing my hand on top of hers. I offered encouraging whispers that she definitely had a bright future.

Just seconds before I was about to leave, the door opened. Ben stood there smiling. On seeing him, unprofessionally I burst into tears. He was standing in the doorway donning a three piece suit. His hair was cut and styled and he was waving the front of his hands towards me. His nails were immaculate. He oozed confidence and

19

self-belief. Excitement raged through the group and they all expressed their surprise and praised Ben on how fantastic he looked.

'You look so handsome,' Cherie beamed, patting him on the shoulder.

'Wow you're gorgeous.' Tracey held out her palms, gesturing towards Ben.

'Oh wow, how good do you look?' I gawped. Ben walked towards me, buoyant. He stared directly into my green watery eyes, his voice firm. He addressed the group.

'Alana said I could do it. I never thought I could but you said I could and I believed you.' He pointed towards me.

I will never ever forget Ben. Had somebody just swathed me in warm blankets? The support I felt in that room at that minute was mind-blowing. My job there was done.

Sunflowers conjure up memories of the rehab and Ben. His determination motivated me. I mustn't give up in my career, I thought, so what next?

Within a month I had accepted a full time job as a domestic violence outreach worker supporting women who were in desperate need of a way to keep safe. I helped by planning protected escapes and gaining accommodation for distressed women who were trying to flee a life of terror.

I couldn't even divulge to my own family where I worked. My work address was a secret, therefore protecting me from potential attacks from dangerous spouses of the women I supported.

Alex always wore smart expensive suits to London. Daily I was clad in leggings and flat shoes or boots - basically comfortable, cheap and practical clothing. I often wondered if I would ever work in a luxury setting. Our lives were absurdly different.

I cannot claim to be materialistic. I worked hard all week and then watched television throughout the weekend. We were in a terrible rut!

DREAMS ARE A CHALLENGE

I arrived home from my trip to the marina.

Pulling my handbag handles high up on my shoulder; I put the key in the front door of our bungalow. Can you guess where Alex was? Oh yes, glued to it. I sat down. The atmosphere was uncomfortable.

I could feel my legs fidgeting in sheer frustration and annoyance, then I blurted loudly, 'So you're still watching this bloody rubbish then?' He glared at me, the sort of evil eyed stare a devil would be proud of. I've seen a boat that I liked. I think we should go to see it tomorrow. I'm fed up with all this crap around here.'

I stared back holding his gaze. I fixed on his eyes until he looked away.

'What the hell are you going on about?' he questioned me, as if he was spitting feathers.

'Pain-in-the-proverbial,' I thought.

'I saw a yacht today. It's for sale. I know it sounds rather bizarre but I want us to go and see it together tomorrow. We need to make some serious changes around here. Everything is a bloody disaster. I can't carry on this way much longer. It's doing my head in.'

He mumbled under his breath that I had gone mad but made no definite decisions. I walked towards the kitchen, pouring a very large whisky and lemonade; then I necked it back. I necked another and fell asleep on the sofa.

Making my way to bed at about 2.30am, I slid into the duvet and nestled down, thinking about the boat.

Sunshine filled the bedroom as we clambered out of bed next morning. We had planned a trip today to Eastbourne to buy a washing machine as ours had decided to churn out smoke, graunch and die.

Sitting in the car, being thrown from side to side as Alex drove in his normal fast manner, I kept on pressing my ghost brake. My thoughts were addled by the boat scenario. Dreamy wishes kept going over in my mind. That could be me drinking champagne on that yacht. What does she have, that I don't? I envisaged lovely chilled fizzy, glamorous, sexy, sophisticated champers in fine fluted glasses filled to the brim with laughter filling the air. That's what I hankered for.

'Once we've bought the washing machine, can we go and look at this yacht?'

I could see by his face he thought I had gone off my rocker. He flicked his eyebrows up and shook his head.

'I think you'd like it Alex. It would be something we could do together.' I tried to convince him.

Silence filled the air yet again as we sped through the countryside. He ignored my comment. Breaking fiercely, Alex swore when a ridiculous dopey pheasant sauntered into our path. Eventually, after much persuasion, Alex agreed to go to look at the boat, despite moaning that it was a ludicrous idea.

'We could look at others too, maybe some which are half the price of this particular yacht?'

I hadn't told Alex how much it was yet and he'd not asked. I had no idea how we would finance it. I hadn't thought that far ahead.

The vision of sipping ice cold champagne in the sun certainly appealed to me. In fact I was in denial with my blissful thoughts about any other matter concerning the boat. But would I be in for a big wake-up call?

Arriving at the Marina, I felt compelled to view the boat but I worried what the salesman might think, 'what are these two scruffy individuals wasting my time for?'

I hadn't exactly dressed for the occasion!

Or was that just how it felt for me? Was I wasting his time? Would we ever buy it? I knew it was a long shot, but to me it was a dream that could possibly come true.

He introduced himself as Bob. His tone was accommodating and keen. Pulling up two chairs at his desk, I launched into a lengthy conversation. I started explaining that Alex had thought I'd gone mad but it was I who was keen to see the boat. Pushing back my hair, I leant forward.

'Can we see some others too? Say about half of the cost of the one over there please.'

'Yes of course. We have two boats moored on the outer harbour. They are about £30,000 but a lot smaller than Water Baby.'

Bob wandered over to the filing cabinet. 'I'll get you some details,' he said, rummaging in the drawers.

I looked around. Over-sized photographs of stunning new boats were carefully positioned on the office walls. Ladies were sprawled over the decks in their bikinis sipping Champagne. This was definitely getting my juices flowing.

My fears of being judged ebbed away when Bob put the details in front of us and flashed a big smile.

In the car on the way here, I had telephoned my sister Kacie to come and have a nose at the boat too. We were still waiting for them to arrive. As we were guided towards the boat, I could feel knots of anticipation screwing up my tummy. Oh such excitement!

'Coooeee.'

I heard a loud scream from a distance. My sister had arrived. Masses of blonde hair were flowing in the wind; her clomping high heels were getting louder as she neared. She hugged me tightly and planted a kiss on my cheek, leaving an imprint of orange lipstick which I tried to rub away.

'What are you up to now?' she asked in a tone that suggested I was being naughty.

'Nothing,' I beamed.

'Come on, hurry up.'

I dragged her by the arm of her soft fake fur coat.

Removing our shoes we all boarded the boat. Lots of, 'OOHH and AAHH,' noises were filling the air.

'It's superb, and it's just sooooo lovely.'

I teetered on the steep steps to go into the galley then backed my way down. A deep mahogany wood met my eyes. I softly touched the edges of the table, which was built to a high standard, with my fingertips. Polished wood was emblazoned throughout and it was a sheer delight. It was just so cute and far better than I had imagined.

The table incorporated a small top in the centre which lifted up for you to put your champagne or wine in. Light green material swathed the lounge area giving ample room for at least six people to sit and socialise comfortably.

A charming narrow galley kitchen displayed a double sink with two huge fridges for the champagne. The gas cooker was gimballed so that it could swing in high seas. Not that I had envisaged high seas as part of my plan.

The boat had two double cosy cabins of good size, one at the pointy end and one at the back, so the boat could sleep six, with two in the lounge.

Opening a heavy door revealed a bright white bathroom. I gazed at the shower and a comfy toilet seat. It crossed my mind that the larger the toilet, the easier it is to plonk your bottom in the right place at sea when it's a bit wavy.

Kacie was grinning at me and I was returning smiles that a Cheshire cat would have been truly proud of. Trying to contain my excitement was hard.

I just kept repeating, 'I Love it.'

25

I was in a dream. I fantasised, for about the hundredth time, that I was the lady who had sat on this very boat drinking champagne. In my mind I was there, the bubbles going up my nose, and I could sense the chilled feeling the drink gave me as I relaxed.

'Are you alright, Alana?' Kacie interrupted, digging me hard in the ribs with her skinny elbow.

'Ouch you. Yes, I love it, don't you?'

Kacie flashed a very happy face in my direction and nodded.

Rubbing my hands in excitement, I became a bit silly and started giggling uncontrollably.

As we disembarked Bob led us along a wooden pontoon, swiping his electronic pass to enter through a couple of wrought iron gates. He showed us towards two further moored sailing yachts I'd asked to see.

Their tired outer appearance put me off before I even got inside either. This told me they had no chance against Water Baby, the yacht we had just fallen in love with, or at least I had.

They were dark and dingy inside and I hated them. We were crouched over, squashed like kippers in a tin. I was only in there for a few torturous seconds. It was nasty and in no way appealing. This one had food crumbs all over the floor and it stank like dirty pants.

'Yuck.' I turned up my nose.

'It stinks!'

Well those viewings were short lived. Have you ever wanted something so much, that it hurts? I just had this sense of longing that I had never had before, a weird feeling that I just had to have Water Baby.

Intense feelings came over me. They were so passionate that there seemed some significant purpose in buying the boat. The champagne monster inside was calling me, or could it be something completely different? I wondered what our boys would make of the boat and if they would like it?

I am thinking of our wonderful children. We have two grown up sons, Joe and Max who are both gorgeous and in their early twenties. Talking to them on the phone is a daily occurrence, despite their ages, and today was no exception.

The faint ditsy tune of my mobile phone sounded. Rummaging in my handbag I found my phone. I raised it to my ear pushing my curls out of the way.

'Hi Max, how are you?'

'Oh hi mum, I just got in actually,' he sniggered under his breath

' I just had a bad situation,' he stated.

'Why what's wrong?' I said sharply.

'Nothing's wrong now,' he retorted, 'I just had the most embarrassing thing happen to me.'

'What Max? What's happened?' I said, thinking of all the worst possibilities.

'I just let the dog out the front door because I didn't have a back door key. Then I led Hooch around to the back garden. Slight problem when I got back to the front door - it had slammed shut,' he laughed.

'Oh blimey, what did you do?'

'Well the thing is, I'd just come out of the shower and all I was wearing was a seriously wet smile and a drenched towel. I went to our neighbour Wendy's house. Her husband answered the door and I was just standing there in a towel, completely starkers.'

I roared with laughter. I could imagine Andrew's face. They are a marvellous couple with a great sense of humour and two sons of similar age to ours.

It was even funnier when Max said Andrew had chosen to make no comment and had just handed him the spare key. Talk about a stiff upper lip and pretending there's no problem, as if everyone turns up on his doorstep more or less starkers!

I then babbled on for five more minutes, telling Max about the boat and how I loved it. He just grunted and politely said he had enjoyed the narrow boat holidays we used to go on and he would look forward to seeing the yacht.

Growing up, I had two older brothers; their antics at times were hilarious fun.

Paul, my older brother, used to hold house parties all the time. As a chubby teenager of about thirteen years of age I can remember drooling over all his fit and muscle bound mates. They were all about twenty years of age.

At one party I recall a wallet went missing and Paul was trying to find it. My brother had them all lining up, as drunk as Lords, and then dropping their trousers in unison. My mouth dropped as far down as their trousers did! That was a very memorable evening. It still makes me smile thirty years on - a row of pert hairy cheeks and rugby players' legs. Oh dear I am drooling?

Early evening loomed at home while we chatted about the day's events at the marina.

'So what do you think about buying the boat then?'

I flinched inwardly waiting for a barrage of disgruntled excuses.

Alex turned and looked at me.

'If we did buy it, then our only option would be to scrape every penny we have in each of our accounts to pay for it. In fact it would leave us pretty much penniless.'

Mulling over the details, we both came to the conclusion that it was just a crazy dream I'd had. When we drifted off to sleep that night Water Baby was laid to rest for the day. For now she was left bobbing about on her mooring, alone in the darkness of the night.

Next morning, lifting my panda eyed head off the pillow; I flattened my curly hair down. It always looked like a stiff toilet brush in the morning until I'd washed it. Alex had left at least an hour ago on his long commute.

LIFE CHANGING EVENTS

I hadn't been up long when I heard my mobile phone spring into life. I had a new text message. Three little words, which were to change our lives, stared back at me, 'I want it.'

Alex was texting about Water Baby.

Smiling to myself I replied, 'If you want it, we should have it. You only live once!'

That's what my mates call me, 'Alana, you only live once.'

'OK let's go for it.'

I danced around the lounge chanting. The deed was done. The right choice had been made; or had it?

Contacting the agent in a fit of excitement, I screamed down the phone to Bob that we wanted to go ahead with the purchase of Water Baby and buy it as soon as possible. He explained to me that we should get a survey completed and that it would be sensible to go out on the boat for a sea trial before we make our final decision.

I cheekily made an appointment for the jaunt the next day and texted Alex to take the day off. I secretly wondered if Bob might have thought that we wouldn't buy it in a million years. So had my call to buy it come as a surprise to him? I never thought I'd be in this position.

I yanked the door open at Ancasta, skipping in with anticipation. I was keen on giving Water Baby a chance to impress us so that we would finally own her.

We set off to sea, donning our life jackets. Oh blimey, it's a bit bumpy I thought as we sailed out from Brighton. Generous waves were slapping at the sides of the boat. Swooping white seagulls decorated the mottled grey skies. I held on tight, the wind whipping my hair across my face.

'Right we'll get the sails out then,' Bob announced enthusiastically. He was very eager to show us the boat in all her glory.

'We'll get the mainsail out first.'

The sail flapped fiercely in the wind. Bob grabbed a winch handle and used his power of strength to wind in the rope, trying to tighten the sail up.

'Next is the genoa.'

The white sheet extended and he tightened that up too. With the sails out he turned the boat further and they billowed out filling with much more air. The boat started to seriously lean over and go to one side.

'Oh blimey! We're going over,' I screamed in the most loud and embarrassing display of shock.

I dug my feet into the flooring of the boat as hard as I could, trying to gain some stability.

'Oh shit! We're going over, we are going to fall in,' I screamed again, my knuckles white.

Did I resemble the scream character? My coat was working its way up my back as I slid off the seat. I thought we were definitely tipping upside down and I would die at sea before I could get my champagne experience.

My heart was pounding and I began gasping in fright. Everyone laughed.

'It's supposed to do that,' Bob reassured me, leaning across. He put his arm around my elbow and tried to help me back up in my seat.

'Is it? Oh shit. Excuse my language but that's frightened me.'

My legs had gone all wobbly; my nerves were shot to bits. I had never sailed in my life before and this was a revelation to me. It was nothing like how I had imagined. The boat was virtually lying on its side. My knuckles stayed white resembling the time I went on a fierce rollercoaster ride in sunny Florida.

I had just imagined a nice peaceful sail and some champagne, not this teeth clenching experience. Bobbing fiercely along the coastline like this was sort of terrifying.

Alex took the wheel. It transpired that he was a natural at sailing. I couldn't even move from my seat. I clung on tight thinking, 'What the blinking hell is going on?'

Sun, sea, surf, wind, terror. The afternoon had gone well. 'This appears to be the life' I thought... if you enjoy nightmares!

It seemed ages ago that we had sailed out into the blue choppy channel. Finally we turned back into the boat filled marina. I was so relieved. I wondered if Bob thought it was exceptionally unusual for someone to buy a sailing boat and not even know it was going to heel over in the wind! Being a virgin sailor, I'd only sailed in my dreams. I had no idea that the boat would tip to one side. My mission was to be that woman drinking champagne, not Elena MacArthur!

I can recall another time at sea which was significantly more humiliating and left me mortified.

I celebrated my 40th birthday in Ibiza. Alex had arranged a scuba dive as a special treat. Plunging between the rocks, I experienced the most wonderful descent. Thousands of red star fish carpeted the ocean floor, something I will never forget. Surfacing from the deep, I was animated about how vibrant and vivacious the vision had been. Ripping off my face mask, I continued to utter spirited babble.

My Buddy smiled at me as he ruffled his wet curly hair. Oh he was quite good looking and I smiled back. It was extremely exhilarating.

'Err Alana, you have the biggest green bogey hanging out of your nose that I have ever seen! It's also spread right across your cheek. In fact it's so big it looks like it's been up your nose for all of your forty years!'

I was mortified. My face turned an incredible deep red, a bit like one of those red star fish. I sunk to my knees and hid my face to wipe away the unmentionable. It was one of the worst moments of my life.

We celebrated with cocktails that evening but I just couldn't get the image of that damn bogey on my face out of my mind.

Sitting back in the sales office back in Brighton with Bob, we agreed for the survey to be done. Providing the inspection showed up no major issues Water Baby would be ours. I sat there looking distressed and dishevelled. Inwardly I felt concerned at what I had just experienced but Alex did not seem to notice.

Days later my foolish desire for us to possess our own boat was fulfilled. There had been a few minor problems identified in the survey but we celebrated with a glass of champagne, and yes it was on Water Baby. My face was a picture as I sipped the cool fizzy drink. I finally had the boat of my dreams but a nagging tension about my reaction at sea continued to concern me.

Jack, the previous owner, had decided to come and show us the ropes. Pardon the pun! Clean shaven with dark brown hair and his mini skirted girlfriend with her young boisterous son followed in tow. Jack was quite well spoken. In the hull, he fished and poked in every nook and cranny that existed. He was specific in showing us every gadget on the boat and fully explained their purpose.

Feeling slightly worried, I glanced about. There was an abundance of instruments and safety equipment on board the yacht which meant nothing to me. Jack stood and explained all about them. They seemed so complicated to operate and the explanations went right over my head. I still had no idea what they did or could do.

Jack had clearly had been an excellent skipper and had made sure the boat was as safe and secure at sea as it could be. Intelligent conversation was taking place and it was all rather formal. Jack and his girlfriend were both speaking with plums in their mouths, putting on a posh act. Unexpectedly, the young lad who was with him sidled alongside us, next to his mum.

'Mum, Jack hurt my bollocks,' I shot a direct glance at him. I was quite shocked but have to admit that a sly smile popped onto my face.

'Shush,' she said pretending not to hear what he had said.

'Mum, Jack hurt my bollocks,' he continued to repeat, getting louder and louder until they threw caution to the wind and asked him what he was on about. It was such an awkward moment but funny watching everyone's faces.

'Mum, Jack pulled my lifejacket up in the air really hard between my legs and he hurt my bollocks,'

He was pointing between his legs with a tiny index finger.

'Don't be ridiculous,' she replied, 'he wouldn't have done that on purpose.' She tried to turn away.

'Yes he did, he did do it on purpose, and he pulled the lifejacket hard and hurt my bollocks,' he insisted. Eventually everyone seemed very uncomfortable and Jack pulled him away from our huddled group, telling him to shut up.

I chuckled to myself, amused at this scenario. It just shows that sometimes, putting on a posh act just doesn't quite work out the way you want. I certainly didn't think it was funny that he'd got hurt but felt it was a little too personal to approach in such a setting. On reflection I was sure it was an accident, I'd seen him just move him to one side.

Finally our tour of Water Baby was over. They left with a big dose of embarrassment, life jackets and everything else he wanted to remove from the boat.

Children can be so funny and their innocence charms me but despite the embarrassment of the moment, I hoped that the little boy was okay.

It made me remember Max, our son, when he was about six and we were out shopping. A bedraggled bird in a cage in the window of a pet shop caught my eye. It had blackened, plucked feathers.

'Oh dear look at him,' I said as I pointed the bird out to the children.

We all stood gawping at this awful sorry sight. Within seconds, I had gone into the shop and bought the cockatiel. One problem was that I had no cage. The ones in the shop were too expensive so I asked the shop keeper to safeguard the bird until I could return to collect him. Scouring the local paper I saw an advert for a second-hand cage.

I was on a limited budget myself. I was watching our pennies!

As we made our way to view the cage I was chatting to my sons Joe and Max.

'I know, I'll make the chap an offer. He wants £15.00 but if I attempt to give him £10.00 cash, I expect he will take it. That's all I've got anyway.'

I continued jabbering away in the car as I drove.

'I have a great idea; I know what I will do. I am going to wave the cash under his nose and hope he'll take it. Yes that's it. I'll wave the cash under his nose.'

Planning my approach, we knocked on the front door.

'Hello,' I greeted the gentleman who directed us all to the cage. I tried hard not to be too enthusiastic, as clearly I wanted it cheaper. I tilted my head from side to side as I looked at it, screwing my nose up a little. Suddenly I felt Max tugging on my skirt.

35

I tried to ignore him and continue buying the smallish enclosure but his tiny hand encased a big chunk of skirt material and he continued to yank at it.

Then it happened.

'Wave the cash under his nose, mum. Mum, wave the cash under his nose.'

He repeated this several times very loudly. It was incredibly embarrassing. My body stiffened and I didn't move. My eyes widened, not really knowing what to do.

'Mum, you said you were going to wave the cash under his nose,' he shrilled.

Red faced I apologised for Max, in between telling Max to, 'Shush.' Luckily the amused man accepted £10.00.

Afterwards I had no choice but to launch into telling him all about the poor bird we were trying to save.

Exiting quickly, I must have left a trail of dust. Uncomfortable yet hilarious, I bet he laughed over that for a long time, just as I still do when I reflect back all those years ago.

My mobile rang. It was Mike at Ancasta.

'Just to remind you Mrs Cowell, all the payments have gone through for the boat. You do realise it is yours now, and congratulations. By the way, when do you want to collect it? It's still here'

'I know. I am on it at the moment.' I laughed.

'Err, there's a slight problem,' I uttered. 'We don't know how to move it. Is there any chance Bob could get it to the mooring once we have confirmation of where she is going to be berthed?' I pleaded.

Silence filled the phone line. I imagined he was raising his eye brows and thinking 'Oh dear, they don't know how to manoeuvre it?' I felt a little silly asking for help.

'Right, when do you think you will have final confirmation then?' he asked.

36

'I'll get back to you as soon as I can once the marina has contacted us,' I reassured him. I dragged my mouth down in a grimace. I was trying not to be a pain in the backside.

'Ok, then we will arrange for Bob to deliver it for you. No problem, just give us a shout when you're ready, OK?'

Mike didn't seem bothered by my 'I can't move it' confession but it left an impression on me.

'Thank you,' I replied, replacing my phone back on the arm of the sofa.

Why had I not bought a yacht before? Maybe it was because I have no bloody idea what to do with it, other than to sit on it and drink champagne. Perhaps because when I stand and look at our 36ft boat, I think, 'Shit, she is massive. What the hell we have done!'

I didn't want Mike to think badly of me as I'd asked for a job at Ancasta selling boats. I'd happily and proudly admitted to Mike I was really good at sales, once selling six bottles of shampoo to a bald headed man!

Bob negotiated the lock to get her out from the inner harbour. He was so confident at the wheel, expertly managing to ease her into our allocated mooring place. Alex and I had sat huddled in the cockpit watching nervously.

Using the heavy weaved rope; Bob tied up the boat so that she would be safe if the wind increased. I watched in awe as he chatted about knots and was kind enough to show us his expertise in tying some of them.

I was unable to tie any successfully.

'Put that round there and pull it through,' Bob said, holding the rope and pulling it towards me.

'Oh blow this lark, I am useless at it,' I said, staring at the mess in my hands.

After several more attempts I discarded the rope on the side.

37

'Got to go now guys, I'll pop by again sometime to see how you are getting on?'

Bob jumped off the back of the boat. I smiled. I thought that he was a great chap. He was, patient, non-judgemental, encouraging and kind.

'Thanks Bob, you've been a treasure. We appreciate your help today. See you soon, thanks.' I waved frantically until he disappeared from view.

Water Baby swayed slightly in the wind. Walking slowly along the pontoon's slatted flooring, I found myself observing her beauty.

I pulled on the side of her with all my might, climbed up and then shuffled down into the hull. Pushing my index finger through the round bored holes, I opened each cabinet and cupboard. I lifted up the plates, cups, knives and forks. Each one had a Beneteau logo on it which I thought was very posh. I raised my shoulders up high. 'Wow, she is ours!'

'Come up here Alana,' called Alex.

'OK, coming.'

Holding onto the thick posts either side of the steps, I far from elegantly emerged on deck.

Alex took my hand, his fingers twined around mine.

'She's great,' he said.

We stood admiring her tethered to her new mooring place. I loved peering to the top of her mast. Excessive excited chat filled the air but one big question which was still to be resolved kept reoccurring. We now have a 36ft French Beneteau Oceanis and we don't know how to sail her.

'So what are we going to do?' I asked Alex.

'How are we going to sail her when we don't have a clue what we are doing?'

We chatted through our options. A local training school called Sailnet offered private tuition.

Over the next couple of days it was my mission to enquire to see if a trainer could come out with us.

I had no idea what trauma, trials and tribulations lay ahead. I had been oblivious to the fact that sailing actually isn't about drinking champagne. So this five ton boat stayed tethered up until we were able to get a qualified skipper to educate us.

LEARNING EXTRAVAGANZA

Dave, our trainer for the morning, turned up bright and early the following Saturday with a rucksack flung over his shoulder. He was a tall gentleman, quietly spoken with a kind face.

This was where our true journey began. Huddled in the hull of Water Baby, Dave decided the first aspect to learn was safety. He launched into a big discussion about the engine.

'Being safe at sea is paramount and the engine must be checked without fail every time you go out,' he stated, looking over his glasses to add serious emphasis.

'WOBBLE, is the word of the day to remember when we do the engine checks. So "W" is for water, "O" is for oil, "B" for belts, second "B" for the bilges, "L" for leaks and "E" for the exhaust.'

Jostling for space, we clambered in the main cabin near the engine compartment. Squashed shoulder to shoulder, we got down and dirty, checked the oil and followed strict instructions.

'Safety equipment is important so put these on.'

Dave lifted up two life jackets, passing one to each of us. Holding it in front of me, I swivelled it around trying to fathom out how to put it on. I put one arm in and then I tugged it round my body hard. As he clipped my belt together, he explained that I needed to keep the jacket a fist's distance from my chest in case it inflated. Apparently it could crush my breasts.

'Oh blimey, flattened boobs are not a good look'

I poked Dave on the shoulder and nervously giggled out of embarrassment. He appeared awkward, ignoring my brash comment and swiftly moved away.

'There's a metal loop on the jacket. Do not panic if a man goes overboard. If anyone does, we will put the motor

40

on, pull the sails in and come back for you. One person will get the job of pointing at the casualty in the water. When we get to you, we will throw a lifeline to you. Grab the line and thread it through the metal loop on your jacket. We can then haul you in. Don't worry as I am sure it won't happen.'

His face softened.

'Now, where's my champagne?' I was thinking. 'Sod the man over board drill. Just give me a bloody drink, anything, whisky, vodka, gin.'

I was worried because it was windy.

Exhaust checked and functioning well, we started to untie the ropes so we could head out to sea.

Dave helmed the boat while I had stirrings of uncertainty as we left the marina and headed out to the choppy, salty waters and as we flopped through the waves, my body tensed up. I felt concerned that when the sails came out I might scream again. There was no doubt in my mind that we were going to be flung over on our side. I knew it would be heeled right over again, just the same as out on our sea trial.

Crashing through the heaped water over each thundering wave, I was clearly frowning. I could see Alex grinning from ear to ear. Dave decided we were far enough from shore to pull out the sails. Her stunning white sheets flapped and filled with air and assertively, Dave tightened them up using the winch handle, showing us how it is done and explaining why.

Over she went. She was gracefully bowing in the wind, giving way to the power filling her sails. She thrust deep into the heaped waves. My heart was bumping hard. To say I felt nervous was an understatement. Why had I not gone to the toilet before we left? I crossed my legs, which is very difficult when you're hanging on for dear life.

'Oh blimey. Sorry but I need the loo.'

I shook my head as I told Dave.

'Don't stay down there too long, you'll get sea sick,' he informed me.

I ventured gingerly down into the heads. That's what they're called. Not toilets but heads. Why on earth are they called that? Trying to undo my trousers was fun. It was as if I had consumed a bottle of whisky. My feet jolted backwards and forwards as we swayed heavily from side to side, the sea lifting and dropping the boat. I leant back, pushing my body hard against the wall.

I lifted the cumbersome lid and plonked my backside down. Whoosh, a big wave hit us side on and I was propelled forward, nearly bashing the top of my head.

I quickly reached out with my left hand, saving myself on the wall. Bang! The toilet seat suddenly bashed down on my bare back.

'Oh shit,' I yelped. I leapt up off the loo trying to rub my back. After another rendition of looking inebriated, I managed to pull up my knickers. I felt queasy.

I expected a big bruise to show for that experience. Oh what fun and still no sign of the champers. Using the palms of my hands to steady myself along the walls, I edged towards the companion way. I grabbed the rails and shabbily made my way back upon deck.

Upstairs Dave explained that a skipper never shouts. Christ I thought, Alex's going to have trouble keeping that one under his belt. He's great but he can get a right strop on if I cock up. I had no doubt, his vocal chords would take a beating during the course of my journey to learn to sail.

With the winds increasing, my hair blew up in the air. I sported a full 240 volts hairdo. Pushing my trainers into the struts of wood on the floor for stability, I huffed. Shivering with the cold and suffering a sense of losing my balance, I was all shaken up.

This experience was definitely made to shatter dreams; if those dreams are of staring sexily into a man's eyes and drinking champagne on a beautiful yacht.

'Oh my!' I thought as I was jolted back into reality. 'What have I done? We bought this boat which cost so much and I am not enjoying myself.'

In fact I was petrified. I briefly tried to remember when I was last as scared as I was at sea today. At fourteen I'd had an operation to remove my bunions. All my toes had been broken and straightened. My parents had taken me to the seaside in my newly acquired wheelchair and a young man had offered to take me for a walk. Plastered from my toes to knees on both legs, I was pretty much bound to my wheels.

He decided that going to the top of a hill, jumping on the back of the chair and propelling me down the steep slope would be great fun. As we were whizzing down, we flew past my parents coming up the hill. I will never forget the look on my mum's face as we sped past. We mimicked a car racing for pole position.

My mum started shrieking and running after us. I was so glad when we came to a halt at the bottom unharmed. I got a right telling off and yet I wasn't responsible for the madness. I honestly thought I was going to die in a wheelchair crash. My heart was pumping as if it was going to explode from my chest.

Back at sea, Dave stated that it was time to go in and boy was I relieved to hear our sail was over for the day.

'Turn directly into the wind to get the sails in. Take all the wind power out of the sails and furl her in.'

Both of us watched as he expertly manoeuvred the bow.

Directly before the entrance of the marina the seas become more disturbed. It was as if we were in a washing machine. Ploughing through the waves back towards the

43

marina, I tried to wave at a young couple who were leaning off the end of the breakwater lifting up their young child.

They waved back smiling, undoubtedly thinking how funny I must have looked, bedraggled and sprawled out across the seat like a weathered scarecrow.

Water Baby rolled and listed from side to side. I hung on tighter. It reminded me of a simulated bull ride in Spain. Have you ever heard of the term 'pulled through a bush backwards'?

I felt sorry for myself. Calm descended as the shelter of the breakwaters engulfed us and I sighed with relief. The marina was my saviour today. I needed a drink.

Inside I was in turmoil. I hadn't enjoyed going to sea today and my mind was going into over-drive. How could I be honest to Alex and verbalise that I thought buying the boat had been a mistake. My perception of owning our own boat had been far from the realms of reality. I experienced an inner feeling of stupidity that I could not express, so I sunk into quietness.

Tying up the boat, turning off the seacocks and locking up the life raft took quite a while. Dave spoke in depth about other safety equipment as we busied ourselves. Soon, she was tidied up; ready for us to leave. We thanked Dave as he left and he agreed to come back the next Saturday.

On the way home Alex enthused about the sail and half-heartedly, I agreed. I just couldn't say what was really going on in my head.

Over the next few weekends, Dave came out and continued to teach us the practical skills. Our friend Robert, also a qualified skipper, had offered to take us out too. Slowly but surely we began to grasp the concept of sailing and how all the instruments worked but I dreaded every sail.

During the many car journeys to the marina, I found myself getting into a state, looking at the trees swaying in the wind and I was asking myself, 'Is the wind too strong? Will the waves be big? Will I die at sea today? By the time I arrived at the boat I had built up in my mind that every sail was going to be a disaster.

Robert was helming the boat and as we ventured out to sea the waves were about 6 feet high. I started complaining that it was too rough for me.

'Maybe you shouldn't have bought a boat. You should have thought twice about buying it,' he bellowed at me. Continuous waves lashed at the sides and sprayed over our heads.

His comments hit hard and I could feel my face redden. I nearly burst into tears. Vulnerable and shaken up yet again, I asked them to take me back to the marina. It was definitely too rough for me.

Starting the engine, then furling in the sails, they eventually dropped me off at the visitors' moorings and went back out to sea. I headed for the nearest warm bar and got myself a large glass of Sauvignon Blanc.

Once again I was sitting on my own but this time my husband wasn't watching sport but out on our boat. I had thought that encouraging him to buy it would bring us closer together but horribly it was all going wrong. Ideas of long romantic champagne sessions were in reality just a dream. I had learnt over the last few agonising months that sailing is a challenging and difficult sport but it had taken £70,000 plus the money to pay for private tuition to discover this.

Each weekend Alex appeared to be getting obsessive about sailing and whilst relishing the experience, I was struggling all the time.

Alex suggested we both train and qualify for our Day Skipper. He handed me a leaflet which explained that there would be five days in the classroom, five days at sea and one night sail.

The courses covered navigational theory, safety and seamanship. I was confused and my emotions were all over the place but I agreed to go ahead and get the qualification. I hoped it would help me build confidence at sea and help me to start to enjoy the sailing, rather than secretly hating it.

On the first day on the course we were settled around a long table that resembled a coffin. I was the only woman in a class of eight men.

As a child I'd hated being at school so I left at fifteen years old with no exams at all. Today I felt similar to that little lost girl all those years ago. I felt insignificant, vulnerable and alone, despite the other people in the classroom.

When I was twenty eight years old, I realised I had a CV with no qualifications and I was embarrassed by this fact. I reluctantly returned to adult education and gained GCSEs in Maths, English and Psychology.

Attending Brighton University a few years later, I engaged in a professional development course. I finally endured some successful education. Today in class I had an odd feeling; I knew I was going to struggle. Being the only woman was bound to cause friction. I could feel the tension before we'd even started.

Everyone was sharing stories whilst the tutor set up. The men were surprised to hear we had bought a 36ft yacht without ever sailing before. Most of the males attending the course had intentions of hiring a boat abroad and getting some experience here in the UK before they went.

Alex excelled in the course content, finding each task second nature. Moving on to the chart work I found it very difficult. Being below average at maths and having to

46

calculate courses to steer was extremely difficult for me. I stared at the maps and figures. They baffled me.

Looking at a typical sailing yacht, we studied the names of everything on the vessel. I was shocked that there were over fifty new words for me to learn and remember. Points of sail came next and how you cannot sail directly into the wind because the sails need to be able to fill with wind to move the boat forward. It sounds simple but in practical terms at sea, it's not so easy.

Tom the trainer explained that some people don't pass the Day Skipper if they can't get this concept when they are out on the water. Laughing, he told us in the past he had failed several people because of this. I hoped this would not be me.

Pieces of string were handed around for us to tie a Bowline knot. No matter how hard I tried, I got into a state, and got it all twisted and round the wrong way. Not one man had trouble. I could see out of the corner of my eye that they were all taking the piss out of me.

'Go home and practice it,' Tom nodded towards me.

'Stupid dick', I thought. I would be able to practice it if I could do it in the first place!

At home I watched Alex confidently tie the knots, whilst I was getting muddled up. I didn't manage it once and wasn't even sure what I was trying to achieve in the first place. Bloody annoying, I thought. I felt so ridiculous. Was being left handed the problem? I just couldn't get to grips with these shitty knots.

'Why can't you do it?' questioned Alex, perplexed at my less than handy work.

'I don't know, do I? I just can't seem to tie the crappy things.'

I thumped the rope onto the coffee table and sat stony faced.

Next day, back in the classroom we covered anchoring, mooring alongside and clarifying all the safety equipment on board. We chatted about the use of different coloured flares in emergencies and how to cope when a helicopter hovers above to complete a sea rescue.

Wow, discovering how many different lights, shapes and buoys there are to signal dangers at night, and routes on passages ahead, had been very interesting.

Being informed that you need a radio licence to use the radio at sea was a surprise, so we opted to get this separately at a later date.

We had been given several questions on chart work for homework. I sat quietly staring at the charts, despondent and clueless. Alex had finished his homework and was laughing at the TV. I'd been trying to knock some sense into myself with a gentle slap on my cheek. I was completely flummoxed by trying to do the chart work. In fact I honestly thought I was going to burst into tears at the table. I sat quietly looking down at the maps in front of me, bewildered. Nothing made sense. I was lost. I was unable to get an ounce of an answer.

Alex huffed a few times in the background. I could tell he was not impressed with me. I heard him make a few comments about how he couldn't understand why I couldn't get it. Getting up from the sofa he came over.

Looming over me, Alex commanded, 'Come on for God's sake Alana. It's so easy just work it out.'

'I can't do it, I don't understand it, and if I did, I would do it wouldn't I?' I defended myself.

Leaning in my face he shouted again 'For Christ sake, just do it!'

I burst into tears but he continued to shout at me. I held my head low and hunched my shoulders over. My thoughts raged. I was so worn out with all this. I had not yet given up but I had continued to try both going to sea

48

and being in the classroom, but I was at breaking point. I thought my head was going to burst.

'Leave me alone,' I screamed banging my fists on the glass table.

Jumping up I ran into the bedroom and threw myself face down into the pillow, sobbing.

My head hurt, my champagne dream now a haunting nightmare. We had spent thousands of pounds. I knew I was losing my husband to sailing and our new boat. I was being left behind.

My eyes were swelling, the tears unrelenting. I was so confused. A few months ago I was quite unhappy but now I was blindingly doomed and devastated because all my hopes and dreams had exploded into destruction. I was severely unhappy.

Angry at Alex for shouting at me, I pulled the worn suitcase out from under my bed. I pulled the wardrobe open and started to throw my clothes in with some still attached to the hangers. Forcing the lid shut, I flopped onto the bed and grabbed my phone.

I texted my friend Julia.

'Hi, do you want to come to Spain tomorrow?'

'Are you serious?' She replied.

'Yes, completely, please come?' I begged, nodding as I pushed the send button.

'I will have to get packed but yes I will come. How exciting. Let me ring you in the morning as soon as I am ready.'

Several texts later all was set. I put the case back under my bed and then spent the evening avoiding Alex.

Later on that night I was sitting in silence on the bed, looking at my hands and thinking. My plan was to wait until he went to work and then get on the internet and book a week in Costa del Sol.

Next morning, smartly dressed as usual, he went to work. Logging onto the computer, an ounce of happiness waded in as I saw the five day weather forecast for that area; seventy five to eighty degrees. So I made a decision that that was where we were going.

I waited patiently for her to call me. My phone vibrated and buzzed.

'Yes all Ok here. I am packed and sorted. What time are you collecting me?'

'I will text you the time as soon as I have booked the flights and hotel.'

I leapt up and ran to the computer. I booked the flights and a four star hotel and excitedly contacted her back.

I left before Alex arrived home. I was gone. Now there was no one for him to shout at. An empty house would greet him tonight and he would be attending the rest of the course for the Day Skipper on his own. I just didn't care at that point.

Arriving at the airport we headed straight towards the bar. She'd been having problems with her hubby so the pair of us ranted about how crap husbands can be sometimes. I expect Alex was thinking the same about wives. Unusually, I found myself mentally exhausted. The last few months had been a major challenge and at this point, one that I had yet to successfully fulfil.

A few drinks on the plane were just the ticket. We were laughing and had left our troubles behind.

'Did that air hostess just give me a dirty look?' I giggled,' nudging Julia. 'I expect she's jealous that I've just ordered my third double whisky and lemonade and she's got to work.'

'You'll be pissed Alana; if you're not careful.'

She elbowed me back.

My whole body relaxed as the alcohol surged through me. I didn't give a damn. I was done in for now.

Alex and I had exchanged a few texts between us but the week whizzed by. Before long I was on the plane coming home, asking for ice in my whisky again.

Julia and I had spent the week just sprawled out in the sun, drinking chilled cocktails by the pool. We'd gone for relaxing meals, walks and enjoyed lengthy chats. Returning home I found that Alex was not amused.

I was sheepish on my return because on reflection I felt that I had behaved in an extreme manner to his outburst. Maybe going to Spain for a week was a bit naughty and a little excessive. At the time, my actions seemed justified.

On the Monday morning the weather was dreary and reflected in my mood. I was fed up knowing my predicament had not changed.

Tied to her mooring the boat sat waiting to be sailed.

Alex had completed his five day theory in the classroom. I hadn't done much thinking in Spain. I had coped by blocking all the crap out. Now I had to consider my next move. What the hell was I going to do?

I telephoned Sailnet who had previously held the training. I confessed, telling them the complete truth and the fact that I had toddled off to Spain.

I explained that I wanted to return to the classroom to try to complete the course. They were brilliant, deciding not to charge me again. They allowed me to return and to attend the classes from the beginning.

I felt self-conscious and uncomfortable as I entered the class. I was the only woman again and this time there was no Alex. Now I really was on my own.

Six men were excitedly chatting when I tip toed in. Within seconds they went silent. After a pause, a few hellos passed my way.

I plonked myself down awkwardly. Thankfully my tutor was someone different. He was from Greece. He wandered over and shook my hand. He came across as a friendly guy. I found his accent a little difficult to understand. His name was Pedro.

I peered around the walls which were bare and the smell of different aftershaves filled the air.

'Right, ah let's a get started,' Pedro smiled.

Some of the course content was easy for me as I had already gone through parts of the syllabus but in the afternoon when we started the chart work my heart sunk. I was still confused and my mind just muddled up.

'Use a pencil and draw a line to where we are going to sail,' Pedro encouraged. 'You do it on the chart which is like a map, working out the bearings to use on the compass in the direction of where we want to sail to.'

Pedro flung his arms out and I grinned at his broken English and theatrical manner which added a bit of interest to the room.

We leaned across the charts which lay spread out on the table in front of us and we all worked separately, drawing and considering the effect of the tide and wind direction on our journey.

Proudly I thought I had finished but as I straightened up in my seat, sheer horror hit me. My ample breasts had been covered in pencil; my white T shirted boobs were now a shade of grey. Had I inadvertently used my bust as a rubber as I tackled the charts? I quickly folded my arms and covered my chest as best as I could, dreading the reaction of the men. I am sure they would be staring at them if they'd noticed. The little devils, and then who knows, I'd probably have been an even bigger joke than I was feeling now.

As soon as the tutor gave more instructions and the men had their heads down, I grabbed my coat and rammed it on, zipping it up in a fluster.

'You going somewhere Alana?' asked Pedro.

'No, sorry I just feel cold,' I said lying. I felt my cheeks flaming.

'Is it cold in here then?' he enquired to the other busy class members.

Confused faces and shaking heads reflected back the opinion that it was warm in the room. I started to sweat almost immediately. Wrapping my ski coat around me had not been a great idea but taking it off wasn't an option either, so stupidly I sat there in silence and suffered.

Part of me wanted to burst out laughing, shout out and tell them what had happened.

'Hey look at my tits guys. Go on, have a good stare. They're covered in pencil. Yes what an idiot I am.' Instead I stayed silent and behaved myself.

'Finish time. You have to go home now please.' Pedro wiped off the white board.

'Thanks Pedro, see you all tomorrow.' I ran out of the class and down the spiral staircase.

Pushing the door open and breaking out, I gasped in the breezing sea air. I felt relieved to get out from the stifling conditions and hastily dragged off my coat. Lord knows what the men would have thought if they'd seen me stripping off.

Long traffic jams greeted me on the way home and I turned up the radio loud, body popping and gyrating in my chair to the beat of the music.

RELATIONSHIPS, EXAMS

Tonight Alex and I would be going out for a curry at a local restaurant.

I returned home late and found him waiting for me. No sooner had we sat down in the restaurant than the firing of questions started.

'What happened today? How did you get on?'

OK. Maybe he wanted to hear that I had messed up. I was cagey about what information I gave him. I'd dragged on a different top on my return home so that his eyes would not zoom in on my pencilled in breasts. Otherwise I may have been a source of amusement.

I heard the owner of the restaurant laughing and as I looked over in his direction he was walking away. He started to scratch his bum. I mean not a gentle scratch but a full on grab your arse and rake it.

'Oh that's disgusting, he's ransacking his backside. How awful.'

I screwed up my face in revulsion. That completely put me off my meal and I left a nearly full plate of food.

Alex was convinced my lack of appetite was because I had encountered a bad day. I just kept repeating that I hoped the owner hadn't cooked my meal after I'd seen him rummaging his bum. It disturbed me, reminding me of another visit to a curry house when I'd found a thick black beard hair in my chicken korma. I'd left my meal on that occasion too.

I got married nearly thirty two years ago. I met Alex in a pub at the ripe old age of fifteen. I'd recently split up with my boyfriend, a kind young man but he was just that; basically a friend. We had been together for some time but I was young and not sexually active.

Standing at the dingy bar, I was in the company of my ex- boyfriend's sister. I was only with her because I had been too scared to tell her I didn't want to go out with her that night. She sported false eyelashes, a severe haircut and had a bit of a reputation as being a bit too easy with the men.

The music was thudding and I was chatting to her when my ex- boyfriend came in. I panicked and went straight over to this complete stranger and grabbed his arm saying, 'If he comes over, can you tell him I am with you.'

I latched on to him tightly, not letting go even when he looked at me as much as to say 'Who the hell are you?'

The pub atmosphere was smoky. It had a basic interior - wooden floors and old furniture; it was just an average boozer.

I could see my ex staring at me holding onto my new found friend.

He told me his name was Alex and we started conversing as if we had known each other for years. Tracey seemed to know the other guy Bret who Alex was with. She was pressing herself up against him suggestively. I felt awkward watching her antics.

After about fifteen minutes she wanted to leave, telling me I had to go with her to another pub. She told Bret we might see them later.

I waved goodbye to Alex. I was really disappointed. We'd had a good laugh and giggle but now Tracey and I were in the cold, walking toward the centre of town.

We stopped off at several pubs and had a reasonable time. We were walking and making our way home when a car tooted like mad and pulled up at the side of us. I could feel a chill run through my body as I feared getting attacked. I wondered who was stopping their car at the side of us but when I gazed through the window I saw that it was Bret and Alex.

Without asking me she leapt in their car and not wanting to be left walking the streets on my own, I clambered in too.

We arrived outside a tatty terraced house. I felt nervous about going in but no sooner had we entered through the front door than Tracey disappeared, thundering upstairs with Bret and leaving me with Alex.

I sat rigid in the shabby chair. He put on some romantic music and moved towards me, taking my hand. I edged out of the chair into his arms. His arms circled my waist and we moved slowly, entwined together. Nuzzling into my neck he whispered in my ear, 'Want to come next door?'

'Why, what's next door?'

I pulled away, gazing into his eyes.

'My bedroom,' he murmured.

I pulled away from him firmly. I was horrified and started to cry.

'I want to go home. I don't want to go into your bedroom. I just want to go home,' I sobbed even more.

Although I'd had boyfriends before they had been just that, a boyfriend. I had had the odd kiss here or there but no bedrooms and no sex.

The more I cried the more Alex flustered. While I was picking up my coat he kindly offered to drive me home. I peered up the stairs as he led me into the hallway, concerned about Tracey, but he told me she was staying the night and was busy.

Awkward silence filled the air as he drove me home. He only spoke to request directions.

Just before I got out of the car he asked to see me again and I agreed, stating that I was happy to go to a pub but not his house.

Getting into my own bed, I was pleased I was home safely. I pulled the soft, warm duvet around me and fell asleep.

Alex phoned me in the morning and arranged to pick me up after work. At that time I was working as a chamber maid.

Marching along when I finished that day, I didn't see Alex waiting for me. I hadn't wanted him to see me looking out for him. I felt uncomfortable and so I put my head down and walked the several miles home.

It was later that evening when the shrill of the phone enabled me to talk to him again. Confused, he questioned me about why I hadn't come over to his car after work. I explained I was embarrassed and shy after balling my eyes out the night before.

Today, sitting in a restaurant thirty five years on, we are still together. Challenges still exist in life but in a completely different form. Now, it is the boat.

Waking up early the next day to attend the course again, I packed my bag and made a sandwich for lunch. I was the first to arrive and decided to try another question out of the exercise book.

Question 9.5
At 0730 UT (log 0.2M) a vessel leaving Shoreham harbour was at Beacon Fl(3) R.11s3M. If a heading of 20 degrees (M) was maintained while the vessel proceeded towards Hamble, what bearing was the direct route position at 0900 UT (log 12.0M)? Additionally, what was its latitude and longitude?

Shit! I am sure I suffer from some form of dyslexia when it comes to sentences and numbers. They just jumble up, making no sense. The charts just sent me into a state. My brain was addled and I was panicking. I kept looking at the question. It was difficult for me to decipher. A few other people arrived and I gave up on the question.

Pedro was serious today; as tomorrow was the day of the exam. No smiles passed his lips and he fired instructions one after the other, expecting us to complete the questions. My pace was much slower than the men and they constantly found themselves waiting for me to finish. Their faces said it all as they anticipated how long I was going to take each time.

I needed a pencil sharpener; as I leant down and picked up my plastic carrier bag it swung towards me and I let out an enormous scream. I had stabbed myself in the leg with the dividers.

Dividers are a metal structure with dart like ends on two points. They are used for working out distance of travel on the charts, but unfortunately they were protruding out of my plastic bag. I had managed to score 180 using the side of my leg.

'Oh shit, that really hurt. I've stabbed myself.'

I was rubbing my leg and once again feeling a bit of a fool. Deep laughter sounded round the room as the men poked fun at my expense. Nasty little men, I thought. I expect they all have small dicks.

Leaving with damaged pride, a sore leg and a stinking headache I headed home. Dreading my return in the morning, I was planning how I was going to cope with the exam.

Pedro informed us that the venue for the exam had changed to a 50ft yacht. It sounded exciting. On my way home that evening I recalled my school days. I'd never been popular, bullied in fact. Being chubby and in a wheelchair fed great fodder for the tormentors. I left school at fifteen, gaining a job in a newsagent in Richmond Upon-Thames.

While serving a customer one day, I was duly marched out of the shop by the local authority school enforcement officers. Leaving school like I did had apparently been against the law. When the date arrived for me to have officially left education, I came away with no qualifications at all.

In my 40s, Alex kindly looked after the children while I went back to study GCSEs. I did two lessons of maths every week, in addition to the course's lessons. I started to make some headway, despite possibly being labelled by some as thick. Eventually, as I said previously, I gained a C in Maths and was chuffed with myself. I continued to take my English GCSE (B), Psychology (B) and Information Technology NVQ2. I also gained my diploma in counselling and went to Brighton University to study Drugs Intervention Strategies so that I could gain another professional development in my counselling. I never gave up.

Next day, when boarding the yacht I stared right up to the top of the mast. It seemed unreachable like the Day Skipper exam. Would I pass? I knew I would get the results today and it was eating away at me.

Pedro had arranged for us to stagger our exams throughout the day. My slot was the first. Sitting at the table on the yacht it smelt new. The interior shone inside and the wood bore no scratches.

My hands were held tightly squashed between my knees. Pedro placed the exam paper in front of me.

'You can start now.'

I sighed as I turned the paper over. Looking at the top of the page, I winced.

Methodically going through the questions, I felt confident on many of them but I still struggled when I was planning a course to steer. I knew I had limited time but did my best to answer them as correctly as possible.

I felt clammy. I could feel my face flushing and getting redder with every step along the way. By the time I had finished, every muscle in my body was tense, my head throbbed and my cheeks burned. I sat still. I was unsure if I had passed. I resembled a beetroot.

Pedro asked me to wait while he went away to mark my work. On his return he sat next to me.

'You have a couple of problems,' my heart sunk; I knew it, I hadn't passed. 'You have a few issues,' he continued and tilted his head to one side.

'I haven't passed have I?'

Then a big smile spread across his gorgeous face,

'Of course you have, well done. There were just two questions which were not 100% but yes, you did brilliantly.'

I wanted to throw my arms around him and squeeze him tight. I was aching with elation and wanted to kiss him on the cheek. I wanted to plant big fat smackers all over his face. Leaving the boat, I felt on top of the world. I had passed.

When I returned home, I was grinning from ear to ear. How exciting it was, I was proud of myself. It was one more step forward. Thinking back, I knew how hard this had been for me and yet I hadn't given up.

Now I had to contemplate trying to get to grips with being at sea in choppy waters. The next hurdle was five days at sea and one daunting night for the practical part of the Day Skipper. Fluffing up my chest and holding my head high, I marvelled to Alex that I had passed the theory. He told me he was pleased to hear my news, I suggested we buy some wine to celebrate and we did exactly that.

MAX COMES TOO

Three days later Alex said our son Max was going to be joining us at sea for the five day practical. I was pleased. A warm fuzzy feeling swept over me now I knew he was coming with us.

Max is 6 feet 3 inches and a black belt in judo and sports a six pack that girls die for. He has the lightest blonde hair and mostly wears jeans and humorous t shirts, just for a bit of fun. In fact some are quite near the mark and I am guilty of buying a few of them!

Since he was a little boy Max has been mischievous. Even when he was in his high chair he would throw chips at me, bash me with his toys and as a toddler run over my feet with his tricycle. One day when he was about 6 years of age he was playing with his brother Joe and his two cousins, Pete and Jason. Their ball had gone over the fence into the neighbour's back garden. All the lads had asked the neighbour to return the ball but he had refused. Joe, Pete and Jason had decided to lift Max up onto the dustbin and told him to pretend he was his dad.

Encouraged by the boys, Max tried to sound like Alex. Putting on a gruff voice, he said 'Hey you penis jabber, give my sons their ball back.'

Max repeatedly lowered his voice and continued, 'Hey you penis jabber, give them their ball back'.

Unfortunately, not only did the neighbour get furiously angry but unbeknown to him, Alex had been stood directly behind him the whole time. His dad had heard everything.

Poor Max was marched up to bed and the boys were reprimanded for making him do naughty things. It is funny thinking about your children, watching them growing up. Life passes by so quickly.

Joe was also a pint sized rascal and once I went into his playhouse and opened the drawers. Lying before me were hundreds of snails. Sadly some had snuffed it. I made him release the live ones and explained that they were living and it had been cruel to put them in the drawer.

When he was older, I was relaxing in the bath, for once. Our bathroom was next to the kitchen. Joe asked if he could put some toast on but what he had actually done was place Melba toast into the toaster and it had caught fire.

He screamed. I jumped out of the bath completely starker's apart from some attached bubbles.

I began bellowing, 'Fire, fire, fire.'

As I ran into the kitchen to put the fire out, the postman's face was squashed against the kitchen window, staring in at the commotion.

Panicking I started to bash the fire with a tea towel and eventually put it out. Covering myself with the tea towel, I shouted to the postman that we were OK. I couldn't get over the embarrassment and yes you've guessed it, next time I saw him down the road, he did have the cheek to say that he didn't recognise me with my clothes on.

Joe was now twenty three, a toned figure with dark hair, gorgeous brown eyes and a handsome young looking face, just like his mummy. Max seemed to take after Alex. He was blonde and wide shouldered and now nineteen years of age.

I was elated that Max was going to accompany us on the Day Skipper practical. It would, for some reason, make me feel more comfortable. I wondered who our Yacht Master might be. If someone was joining us for several days at sea, I hoped they would be good fun.

The week before our venture at sea arrived, it was my job to do the victualing for the boat trip. Victualing is providing food and provisions for the week ahead to make sure we can survive on the boat without having to leave our vessel to get more grub.

At home I was frantically stirring, boiling and baking. The kitchen steamed up. Cooking a fresh lasagne and spaghetti bolognaise meant they could go in the oven on the boat to reheat. I also bought some frozen food: vegetables, potatoes, milk, bread, cheese, ham and some cereals and not forgetting lots of lager, wine and a bottle of champagne for the moments that we could chill out. At least that's what I hoped for.

On the Monday morning we were on Water Baby. I had made sure that she was clean and her wood polished to perfection. Providing a warm cabin for our guest meant that poor Max was expected to sleep in the lounge area of the boat and, to be honest, I wasn't too happy. Being so tall I knew he would struggle for comfort and his long legs would dangle over the end of the bed.

Wondering who our trainer would be for the next week was a daunting prospect. What if we didn't get on and what if he was horrid?

In the distance we could see a chap walking up the pontoon towards us. He was carrying a big rucksack on his back and was an older man. Plonking his bag on the deck floor, he introduced himself as Gordon. He was well spoken and told us we would all do as we were told or there would be consequences.

I took an instant dislike to him and thought, 'fussy fart'. He came down and helped himself to the bow cabin. I turned my nose up. I shot Alex a glance that said 'Bloody hell. This is so not going to be fun'.

I tensed up straight away. He was like a sergeant major. I desperately wanted to pass my practical exam but as soon as he'd spoken, I had made up my mind I was in for another nightmare.

'They'll be no slacking over the rest of the week,' Gordon boomed.

Max looked at me smiling, knowing I wasn't keen. Laid back, chilling as usual, he repeated, 'Yes mother, no slacking.' He made me giggle.

Max is such a relaxed character. He even slept through an earthquake in Zante. The earth shook so much that the water in the swimming pools were flopping over the sides. Large buildings swayed but he carried on snoring until I screamed, banging on the door of his apartment to wake him up.

Max got on well with Gordon, striking up lengthy conversations. Above deck it was raining and quite windy. On the way back from the toilet block a fellow sailor decided to tell me it was force 5 today, up to 21 knots of wind, so it was going to be rough at sea.

Clambering back on the boat, I spoke to Gordon, raising my concerns about our first day and informing him of the conversation I'd just had. He explained that we would venture out regardless and that when you go sailing you always have to change your plans, according to the conditions.

Not what I wanted to hear. Staying here would have been my preferable plan.

Despite the weather, and knowing the sea was fairly rough, after our WOBBLE checks we tightened our life jackets ready to set off. Just before leaving we completed a radio check.

'Solent coast guard, Solent coast guard, Solent coast guard, this is Water Baby, Water Baby, Water Baby, radio check on channel six-seven please. Over.'

'Loud and clear Water Baby. On channel six-seven.'

'Thank you, Water Baby. Out.'

I replaced the handset.

Exploding the bow of the boat into the waves, we headed towards Chichester.

Our faces peered through the hoods on our warm sailing jackets as the rain lashed our skin. Chilled but with flushed cheeks, we sailed along. I hated it and within a few minutes wanted to go to the toilet. I just kept holding on, as I didn't want to go down into the hull of the boat in the awful conditions. I felt in a permanent state of alertness, and tension surging through my body. I wanted to perform one hundred per cent to gain this qualification.

As the weather worsened, Gordon gave orders that we were going to sail to Shoreham rather than Chichester. It was the next place of shelter. Max seemed at ease. Alex was focused on the way ahead and I clenched my fists in my pockets. He advised us to prepare for when we arrived at Shoreham because he had plans for us to reverse the boat and learn how to anchor in the calm of the harbour.

In the distance we could see the chimney at Shoreham looming. We knew the bigger the stack looked, the closer we would be getting to our destination.

Gordon gave us his expert guidance on anchoring. 'Think, always consider what lies ahead, and ask yourself questions like: will we be sheltered? What sort of protection do we have from the wind? Is the tide, or are other vessels coming in?'

His eyes shot towards us all as he continued, 'What is the sea bed like? Consult the charts to see if it is shingle, or are there rocks that could be a hazard to us. If we want a good anchor holding, then mud and sand give a better grip than shingle or rocky bottoms.'

His voice was stern and he reminded me of my granddad a little bit. I didn't seem to be gelling with him at all.

Gordon looked at me.

'What else do you think we need to consider,' he asked confidently.

Rubbing my forehead, he waited for my reply, 'Making sure we have enough room to swing. If other boats are anchored near us too, it could be dangerous.'

'Well done Alana. Yes we need to be accurate, so that we are not going to swing on the anchor in a big circle and hit another vessel.'

Grinning, I was pleased I had said something constructive and correct.

'Chain length and warp is very important when anchoring. In general you need to find out how deep the water is and when using chain you let out 4 x the depth. With warp, you let out 6 x the depth. But remember the amount of water under us will change with the rise and fall of the tide.'

Gordon showed us a book and it had five pictures of different types of anchors and their names in it. Apparently Water Baby had a Dane Forth.

Despite misty rain and choppy waters we finally arrived at Shoreham. It was mid-tide but heading towards low tide. Trying to work out how much depth we had was fun. Not! As the tide was going out we had to try and work out what the lowest astronomical tide would be that day and if we were going to run aground. Between us, we managed to work out that we wouldn't be able to stay anchored for too long as we would eventually hit the bottom in a couple of hours.

I was fraught.

'Are we going to be OK? We aren't going to crash the boat are we?'

Gordon seemed so chilled, 'We'll be fine.'

Since buying the boat we had not used the anchor and it was a worry if it would even work.

'Ok, you are all going to lower the anchor and have a go at the helm too.'

Dropping the anchor was done by pressing a red button up on the bow and then the anchor slowly lowered into the sea.

The person at the helm had to reverse the boat calmly as the chain started to lie on the ocean bed. We all stood watching, hoping the anchor took hold. I wasn't calm at all. I was stressed and shaking as I reversed the boat. Worry, worry, worry. That was me.

Max lowered the anchor and once we had established it had a good hold on the bottom, he then pushed a grey button and up came the anchor creaking on the chain. It was dripping with smelly seaweed and his face was a picture while he tried to drag the sloppy goo off and chuck it back into the sea.

Pouring with rain, the weather was horrid, despite being the first week of August. Unfortunately this was supposed to be our summer. It was a complete washout.

'Right your turn on the anchor Alana,' Gordon boomed.

I held on tightly as I made my way to the bow of the boat and straddled the chain locker ready to press the buttons to operate the anchor. I gritted my teeth as I tentatively pushed the button and the anchor started to lower. In fact it was easier than I thought it was going to be. Upon lifting the anchor I was lucky that I didn't have to pluck off seaweed like Max had done.

Alex took his turn and everything went smoothly but as time was moving on we needed to go into the lock and get through to gain a mooring with shelter for the evening.

Radioing ahead, the Harbour Master said they had no moorings left and that we were going to have to raft up next to other vessels. Straight away my nerves were on edge. What if we crash the boat? How are we going to do this?

Gordon took control explaining that as we go through the lock, we need to all look for boats we can go alongside and then we can tie onto someone else's boat.

We left the lock and trundled down the marina. It was packed. Row after row of boats were tethered together.

Gordon announced we were going to tie onto the end of four other boats. This meant we would be the fifth boat out. It was mind boggling. He informed us that we needed to tie several ropes together with a bowline knot so that we could get two lines from our boat back to shore.

I panicked. I didn't even know how to tie a bowline, so I snuck up to Alex and whispered to him to take control of tying the ropes. As we came alongside another sailing boat we tried to grab onto the cleats with our ropes and tie her on. By clambering over other people's boats we finally managed to tie her up,

I hated it. I felt out of control and didn't want to let on I couldn't tie a bowline. I was hoping my lack of proper knot tying would go unnoticed.

Gordon directed us with the rules of mooring alongside. We mustn't cross the back of someone's boat; we had to make sure we only went round on the bow, therefore not encroaching on people's personal space.

Feeling smelly, we all decided to go to the shower block and freshen up. The toilet blocks were disgusting, cold and dead spiders hung from old webs. I hadn't enjoyed today. It had been wild at sea, wild mooring and wild in the showers.

I had been allocated to cook for the evening but the good news was that Max and Alex also had to take their turn this week, so therefore on the plus side I was going to relax for the two following nights.

Gordon was pleased to sit down with a cold beer and Max and Alex cheerfully joined him. I sipped a heavenly chilled glass of wine and my thoughts whirred about what tomorrow would bring. I reheated the spaghetti bolognaise and cooked the pasta. We feasted on garlic bread topped with freshly grated cheese. Sounds of satisfaction echoed through the hull.

Feeling full and warm my mind just kept going round and round, worrying about what would happen on day two. After a few glasses of wine and several beers later we all clambered into our beds. Max's feet hung right out from the bottom of the seating area where he'd laid down to sleep. I tried to tickle them. Kicking out, he was not amused. I could hear him huffing and puffing as we all settled down for the night.

Waking up I groaned, another day. Gordon rammed the almanac under my nose and insisted I worked out the tide for leaving Shoreham as today we were heading towards Chichester.

I had briefly used the almanac in the classroom. It gives all the times of high and low tides for every day. It also explains entry details about the port or harbour and limitations of each lock. Each explanation is abbreviated and can be very complicated.

I decided we could leave and as we prepared to cast off, we contacted the Harbour Master who proceeded to sternly tell us off. We were going nowhere as I had miscalculated the tidal height and our boat would not go through the lock without dragging the cill with us. I was so embarrassed. Here was my first big mistake and it could have meant a crushed boat and many red faces and a possible fail with the Day Skipper course.

Gordon sat down with me and discussed where my calculations had gone wrong. I was trying to make excuses but I had to admit my dismal failure to calculate correctly. I felt I had let everyone down. I tried to keep positive but was feeling incredibly stupid and concerned I would now fail.

Informing us it would be at least two hours before departing, Gordon decided to make us all take the helm and start practicing coming alongside the dock. Heading towards the concreted wall we had to turn the boat on full lock to enable this 36 feet beast to gently settle against the land.

I needed a whisky on my attempt and I am sure I must have looked like a cat in headlights as I turned the wheel.

'Gently, gently,' Gordon encouraged, 'and now hard down on the lock.'

If I hit the boat on the concreted wall Alex would be angry. I glanced at Alex. He was in a dither, his head raised up high, his eyes were wide.

I could tell he was thinking, 'we are going to crash!'

The fenders hit the wall and they did their job of protecting the side of the boat.

'Yes, Yes,' I screamed like it was a scene from the movie When Harry Met Sally. I had done it. Alex and Max were securing the ropes on shore. I was so pleased with myself I beamed.

He said it was a perfect landing. I also had to practice reversing and that was far from fun. I was pretty useless and the boat wandered all over the place. I couldn't seem to master it.

Max and Alex managed to come alongside and reverse in a controlled manner. Secretly this annoyed me as it came naturally to them, where everything I did seemed to be a major struggle.

Great news. Two hours had passed and we were able to head out to sea and make our way to Chichester. Dull skies lay before us. Slightly calmer seas were a welcoming sight after yesterday's stormy weather.

Max had wrapped himself in a single duvet and laid down on deck. Chill out time again for him and yet I still seemed like I was on a knife edge. Gordon asked me to go down and sit at the chart table, setting a task for me to plot a course to steer to Chichester. I was downstairs for about 30 minutes and beginning to feel seasick. With the gentle roll of the waves, my sense of awareness frazzled and my brain was becoming confused.

'Actually, I am not feeling very good. Can I go up on deck?'

'OK, you've done quite enough and worked it out well, so up you go'.

I clambered up the steps into daylight and I sat down. Max burst out laughing at me. I was a little green. In my mind I knew that they too would have to go down at some stage and it would be my turn to laugh at them. Terribly unwell, I started to be sick over the side of the boat.

'Make sure you do that downwind,' Gordon hollered. Oh dear! I just wanted to be on land, but we had many more sea miles to go. I couldn't concentrate on anything other than the fact I felt so ill that I was vomiting. I wanted my mummy.

Several hours later we could see the West Pole near the Chichester entrance but we had a problem. There were hundreds of yachts and dinghies taking part in a regatta. It was worse than the M25. Sailing right between all of them, Gordon decided we were all going to have a go at the helm, dodging them.

Alex was first to take the wheel and when I say hairy, it was completely mad. Dinghies were darting like fireworks behind us, in front of us, at the sides of us. Alex's face was crinkled. The concentration and big frown said it all. How we didn't hit the dinghies I have no idea but sail through them we did. Max grabbed the wheel and there were lots of 'Oohs' and 'Ahhs,' big smiles and laughter. It was better than a computer game. This was the real deal.

It was my turn next as I took the wheel I was shitting myself. I didn't want to hurt anyone. Running the wheel through my hands I negotiated my way through the splendid show of sails. My seasickness faded into the background as I got stuck in and continued through the maze of coloured sheets.

It was an experience that will stay with me forever because despite the challenging situation it was incredibly beautiful and a wonderful sight.

Getting near misses every second meant it was hair raising stuff. When we finally got through the regatta we were all full of relief but absolutely chuffed we had all done brilliantly. For beginners it had been pretty difficult.

Smiling faces filled the cockpit and Gordon had been impressed with our determination. Did we have a choice?

Edging our way down to the marina, we had to radio ahead and book a space for a berth for the night. As we were already berth holders at Brighton we didn't need to pay for the mooring tonight so that was a big bonus.

Oh no! The lock that needed to be negotiated appeared daunting and Gordon told me to take the helm and manoeuvre her into the available space. I managed to bring her in slowly. I couldn't believe it was me at the wheel. We waited patiently until we were told where we could find our allocated mooring. I had a mini panic and asked Max to take over. My confidence was taking a nose dive. No way could I reverse her in. I was proud of my son as he managed really well. We tied up.

Tonight it was my turn to relax and watch Max cook the dinner. Settling down we all grabbed a cold drink.

Going over what we had achieved today was really satisfying, having completed many aspects of the course already. Unfortunately, I continued to feel I may have failed due to this morning's major cock up. I had started to warm to Gordon. I really had taken an instant dislike to him. His demanding voice had freaked me out, reminding me of my granddad.

My thoughts that it would be a complete disaster were unfounded. I still laboured through all the tasks but thankfully didn't feel he was as judgemental as I assumed he was going to be.

Snuggled up at the table, Max dished up the meal he had cooked.

I was thinking about the time when we were skiing in Austria and the food was glorious. Max and Joe were at the table when Joe asked his dad if he was enjoying the sausage roll soup. Alex replied, 'Oh yes, it doesn't offend my palate.'

Max and Joe, two teenagers at that time, nearly fell off their chairs with laughter.

'Offended palate,' they both repeated and giggled.

They found Alex's terminology very funny and for the rest of the holiday made fun of his comment every time we sat down for a meal or snack.

I remember my friend Megan in a restaurant starting to choke. She was really making a meal of it, spluttering, coughing and croaking, so I ran behind her and started smacking her on the back. She continued apparently getting worse so I came up behind her and tried to do the Heimlich manoeuvre, lifting her up in the air and using my arms under her chest area.

Suddenly she gasped, 'It's a chilli. It's a chilli.'

She wasn't even choking. It had been a hot chilli she was chewing.

'What a drama queen,' I screamed at her.

Red faced she started to drink tons of water. Honestly I thought she was dying.

She is so dramatic sometimes and once when we were playing water polo, she was performing, slapping her hands all over in the water, shouting and screaming for help as if she was dying. Wading quickly through the water to help her, I lifted her up getting her head out of the water and held her upright asking her what was wrong, only for her to say she had cramp. I let her go. I was very cross with her as I genuinely thought she needed an ambulance.

Max's dinner was great and we decided we would go and have a few drinks in the yacht club. Toddling off together we had a great evening full of laughter and fun.

We chatted about boating and how we used to hire a narrow boat every year. Our holidays were always full of adventure. We took our black Labrador with us one summer. Tying up by a beautiful sheep laden field and right by the side of a local pub, we were able to get some water and Alex was filling the tanks. Hooch, our dog, had run off up the path and over the bridge.

I had gone to try and bring him back, running after him. He scampered into the distance so I was now on the other side of the canal. I could see Alex looking around him, when he thought Hooch had disappeared. He didn't see me run after him, and then he started to scream at the top of his voice pointing at a Labrador dog on the next boat.

'Hooch! Get back here, get back here. What are you doing on that boat Hooch?' He continued shouting at the top of his voice and I could see the man staring at him on the next boat, looking down at the dog.

Alex carried on and I started really laughing. The dog he was shouting at was brown not even black and the owner was looking at Alex as if he had gone stark raving mad. I started shouting back at Alex that I had Hooch. It was hilarious. Everyone was laughing. Alex went over to the owner of the other boat and apologised profusely. He decided that day that maybe he did need glasses.

While chatting on Water Baby after a few drinks at the yacht club, I decided to tell Gordon about Max's pre-school visit when he was about to start school. We had spent the day at the school but on returning home Max cried and cried, saying he did not want to go back anymore. I couldn't seem to get the reason out of him. Eventually he told me, 'I didn't like that man.'

The only man we had seen was the headmaster.

'Why sweetheart, what's wrong? Why didn't you like him?' I gently stroked Max's forehead.

'He had hair coming out of his nose. It was coming down like a black spider,' he snivelled.

It cracked me up so much. I tried to persuade him that some men do have hairy nostrils but they are OK really, even if rather unsightly. I couldn't console him about the nose hair and the first week of school was a real challenge getting him used to the dreaded conk hair.

I have to admit the only thing I noticed over the next few years when talking to the headmaster was his nose. It did have the impression of a tarantula hanging out. From a child's eye you could see it was more than a little scary.

On day three of sailing, the sun was shining and today we were venturing along to sail from Chichester to Portsmouth and from Portsmouth to Cowes on our night sail.

Leaving Chichester I was asked to take the helm and emerging from the lock I suddenly felt the boat jolt hard. We had run aground. I panicked and started to bellow, Gordon told me to calm down and to try to reverse the boat.

'But if we move backwards won't the boat dig in even more?'

I was flustered and I thought I was going to fail.

75

'No, just do what I say and we should be OK'.

I gingerly put Water Baby into reverse and gently she began to ease back and become free.

Off we went again but I was shaking so much I gave the wheel to Max.

As we moved along it felt like we had hit a speed bump. There was a big bump and we all groaned.

'Ohhh what was that?'

Again we had run aground. I was livid. What are we going to do?

Gordon advised Max on how to manoeuvre her out and whilst we were all very nervy we did get going again.

While checking the weather would be in our favour for a night sail, excitement and apprehension flowed through me. Tons of tasks were on the agenda today and before we departed Chichester we had a full cooked breakfast. It had to keep us going until early evening.

On the way out from Chichester we had to navigate through yet another regatta. With tense, white knuckles again, each one of us took turns to negotiate these whipping wonders.

Conditions at sea were fairly windy so the waves hit the bow hard and slamming noises whistled through the air.

On passage we discussed collision regulations and rules of the sea with regard to giving way to other vessels. Reading the training manual we also covered leading lights, pilotage plans, transits, knots and lights on boats for night sailing. Chatter filled the air and soon we could see the Spinnaker Tower at Portsmouth.

I screamed with delight at a seal bobbing up and down who welcomed us to Portsmouth, his big beautiful eyes peering above the water line. He was gorgeous. I'd never seen a wild seal.

Motoring into a large clear area, we agreed to start the man over board drill. Gordon declared that we would throw a fender over the side of the boat and work as a team to get the inflatable back on board. We poked and prodded to find the most inflated fender so it was nice and big like a body. Flinging it over board I grabbed the hook and leant over the side of the boat trying to stretch as far as I could. Alex helmed the boat and had turned her round. Making our way alongside the fender I was able to hook it quickly and bring it back on board. I was struggling and the muscles in my arms were shaking. I hurled it back on board. If it had been a real person, this would have been a nightmare. I just wouldn't have had the strength to get them back on board. I am afraid they would have suffered severe cold, be drenched and half dead, so if I ever get my Day Skipper and go to sea, I pray no one ever goes overboard, especially in the winter!

Max and Alex managed to complete the man over board drill brilliantly and I was pleased with myself on this occasion.

Gordon suggested we drop anchor and rest for a while before our evening sail. Glistening twinkles reflected on the sea from the sun and I felt quite warm, huddled in the cockpit.

Max was talking about funny situations and I recalled the day we went for a nice walk in the countryside. Bearing in mind Max is over six foot tall, we had been trundling along over stiles when I shouted to him to jump on my back. He was laughing loudly as he wrapped his legs round my waist. I held his legs tight and started to try to walk with him bouncing up and down.

Despite being imposing he was incredibly light and with each step I gained momentum. He started to plead for me to put him down but I continued.

'Mum, let me down,' he was bellowing over and over again. I was laughing and wouldn't let go. It was funny; an eighteen year old travelling on his mother's back, him shouting, me hysterical with laughter and him booming that he didn't want his mates to see him in this predicament.

After quite some time I eased his legs to the ground. I was out of breath and he wasn't happy but did break into a wry smile when I continued to hoot with laughter into the air.

Gordon chuckled as we reminisced. I also remembered when, as a little girl on a camping holiday, I decided to put my dad's false teeth into my mouth. I really rammed them in but it was about 5am and everyone else was asleep. I pushed and pulled trying to get them out but they were stuck fast and I couldn't speak. All I could do was make chesty grunting noises.

I had to wake my parents and when my father had seen what I had done he was really angry. My brothers and sister awoke and became frenzied with amusement. Their sister looked like a demented Cheshire cat who had also started to bawl when clearly the teeth just were not budging and dad couldn't remove them either.

It was a trip to the A & E department, where a very stern doctor announced the remedy had to be a general anaesthetic to get them extracted. Although I was only very young I can remember how much my jaw ached for days afterwards and the pain I'd encountered on the trip to the dreaded hospital. Max had heard this real life drama several times but Gordon seemed to find it hilarious, smoothing his hat over his head.

My mind was racing over funny incidents I'd had during my life and I recalled the raucous evening we enjoyed for my friend Charlotte's hen night.

'Alana, I don't want anything tacky for my hen night,' Charlotte had warned me.

Being cheeky I turned up with a medium sized box. Now this package had not been opened. It was sealed but it said on the outside, 'Dare to open me, if you dare'.

Charlotte sat staring at the box whilst she enjoyed several drinks. Now in my eyes I had not bought anything tacky along. It was nothing more than a box but the contents were tacky. It was up to her if she wanted to open it.

Funnily her curiosity got the better of her and later after a few more bevvies in the pub she opened the box up. First she pinned the L plate on her back, then blew up a rubber ball and chain and attached it to her ankle. After drinking more champagne in the mini bus, she read through the list of dares. One of the goads included a soft hairy pussy (a soft, furry cat toy) and later on in the night club I watched her parade around lifting her pussy up to twenty strange men. The challenge was she had to ask twenty men to stroke her soft hairy pussy.

Normally Charlotte is so lady like. It was one of the most side splitting things I have ever seen. Even funnier after her asking the men was when they all started to actually stroke the pussy, sometimes with just one finger gently over its head.

The evening ended up with an ultimate dare to the whole group. Who could win by performing the biggest fake orgasm?

Twelve of us girls were stood on the promenade of Brighton beach making the most horrendous noises but we were all laughing so much we never concluded who had been the rudest and loudest.

Zoe was also standing there with a big rubber willy poking out of the zip of her trousers shouting 'I've got a big one,' whipping her hips from side to side so it slapped

79

about. Several years later we often giggle at our antics that night. Naughty at forty was the rule. I am blessed with great friends.

Looking around the beautiful mooring, seagulls flew gracefully, swerving through the high masts which were waving in the breeze. Mottled skies entwined with the high air trails left by jets possibly bound for warmer climates. Occasionally the seagulls screeched with excitement as some young children threw bread into the air for them.

Alex had to cook today and so he was busy preparing the dinner. Tonight we would be catching the tide to sail to Cowes. I was feeling anxious about the night sail. We had discussed lights at sea on vessels and on markers warning us of danger points on our planned passage but I imagined it was going to be scary, dark and an experience to take really seriously. If anything went wrong I didn't want to be stranded in the sea in the pitch black.

Alex served the meal we had all been patiently waiting for and we continued to chat. An aeroplane flew low, disturbing our peace. It appeared to be a fighter jet and the roar was ear splitting.

After dinner Gordon recommended we tie some different knots. I was still useless. It didn't matter how hard I tried, it was still boring, and even if I managed it once, I wasn't be able to do it again unless I was shown.

Max shook his head as he watched my antics.

'Mother, what are you doing?' He laughed.

I looked across at him guiltily as if I was terrible for not being able to achieve the bloody things.

'I can't help it Max. My brain just won't work it out however hard I try. It's not happening'.

Gordon was smirking at me and I went as red as a cherry. It was all rather embarrassing yet again.

Night fell and we prepared to set sail. Donning hats, gloves, warm coats and our life jackets we released the lines from the mooring ball. Max took the helm.

It was fascinating looking ahead as the lights around the harbour reflected off the water. A dull humming filled the air from the engine as we motored along and the atmosphere was electric.

Within seconds our whole boat lit up from behind. We all shot around, quickly looking behind us. We were in for the shock of our lives!

A massive cruise liner was coming straight at us. It was like a block of flats quickly approaching towards us, shining a bright spotlight onto our vessel to warn us of its presence.

I screamed, 'Oh Max! Quick, get over, get over'.

Max turned the wheel to the right and put the throttle on full for speed. We were all willing our boat to get out of the way. I will never forget the look on everyone's faces as we saw the vessel looming in the dark. I am sure I wasn't the only one shaking in my shoes. Max coped so well and Gordon was keen to tell us that we needed to learn from this incident, that not only should we watch the way ahead but we must keep a look out behind us too. Not one of us had bothered looking at our rear and even Gordon was quite surprised that we had not heard the engine from the large ship.

'Pride of Bilbao' was the name of the liner and as she made her way past us, I was amazed by how colossal she was. We craned our necks to see the top of her and saw several people waving as they passed.

Gordon then informed us that a few years ago this enormous ship had been investigated about an incident involving a yacht and that the crew had died in this accident. He believed there was an inquest but was not sure of the outcome.

We continued out to sea and I was now constantly looking behind our boat to make sure we didn't miss anything else steaming towards us. I noticed that Max and Alex kept a good watch out too. We had made one mistake none of us ever wanted to repeat again.

Identifying boats ahead by using their lights, we could work out their direction of travel and approximately what size they were. Hazards ahead were identified by cardinal buoys of which there are four types: North, South, East and West. At night each cardinal flashes differently to identify where the hazard is.

The night voyage was peaceful and thankfully, never again as eventful as the start. A beautiful black sky twinkled with stars and it was magical. The sea was not rough either and as we gently sailed along I was in awe. Sailing at night was stunning.

We were able to moor on a visitors berth when we arrived at Cowes. Gordon said someone would be along in the morning to get our fees to pay for it. I was so relieved to get back on land even though the experience had been quite wonderful, and when I climbed into bed I went fast to asleep.

Next morning we were going to sail to Hamble for lunch, but not before paying for our stop at Cowes.

We concluded that the RNLI were practicing sea rescues as a helicopter hovered for ages, lowering and lifting someone from the sea. I watched the capers as the wind whistled through the masts and pooing seagulls perched on the pylons. I could smell the sea air and a few large fish swam at the side of the boat feeding from seaweed. I felt so tired. I just wanted to go back to bed but that was out of the question because we were on a tight schedule.

Max was sitting opposite me and I remarked, 'I wish there was a supermarket where you can buy bodies, heads, arms and legs. I need new everything. I am aching from head to toe'.

Max called me old and twiddled his fingers. He looked down, slyly thinking his mum was going to give him a playful bash.

'Cheeky little devil.' I retorted.

'I wish I had the wisdom and experience I have now but I want the body of an eighteen year old,' I announced. Max grinned.

'Old fart,' he uttered.

This time I did get up and playfully cuff him on his blonde hair.

Sitting down, my mind wandered back to a conversation I'd had with my friend Penny.

'We're getting old. We don't go out to do anything anymore, do we?' I stated.

Penny smiled.

'In a fortnight there's a male strip night at the Broadway in Uckfield.'

'Why don't we go? I agree we've got old girl. We don't do much these days?' I encouraged her.

She tilted her head. I was patiently waiting for a reply. 'OK but can we just say to our hubbies we're going to a craft night or something? I just don't want to tell my husband that we were going to see men whipping their clothes off. It just doesn't feel right to me,' she grinned.

Two weeks later, we crept naughtily out of the house for our supposed craft night.

Bustling, noisy chatter filled the night club. Loud music blared into our ears as we pushed our way right up to the front where the action was going to be.

The strippers were very lively, gyrating their hips to the music and thrusting their pelvises towards the screaming women. Penny and I were waving our arms up towards the strippers. Talk about having a ball! After a few more drinks we were getting even rowdier and livelier.

We had a fantastic fun filled evening dancing along to the music, reaching up to the strippers, swaying from side to side. When we got home we both slipped into our beds and fell asleep in an alcohol induced slumber.

The next day Penny telephoned me and screamed down the phone to ask me if I had seen the local Argus newspaper.

'No, why?' I enquired.

'Alana! We are both on the front page of the Argus. The headline says, 'Strippers come to Uckfield' and there is a picture of you and me, our arms upstretched to the strippers. Honestly, you can see it is us and we are bang smack in the middle of the photograph,' she wailed.

'Oh bloody hell,' I screamed back. 'I'll have to go and get a copy of the paper. I have no idea what to say to Alex.'

I put the phone down and drove frantically to the shops and there I was on the front page with Penny. Now how was I supposed to explain this one?

Back home, when Alex arrived in from work, it was confession time. Luckily he found the funny side of it but let's just say the village gossips had something to talk about!

Alex and Gordon sat at the chart table plotting today's sailing. Max and I just relaxed on deck waiting for some instructions.

'How long have you and dad been married mum?'

'Err I'm not sure. I think it's about twenty eight years.'

'Where did you go for your honeymoon?'

'Oh don't start me on that Max. It was the most awful event ever.'

'Why, what was wrong?' Max frowned.

'Do you really want to know?'

'Yes I do mum. Did dad misbehave?' he grinned cheekily.

'Our honeymoon should have been one of the happiest times of my life but in fact it was one of the worst. Our wedding was done as cheaply as possible with homemade wine for the tables made by my dad. He then announced to your dad's mum at the table that he had not even tasted the wine, to see if it was acceptable. Nan was not amused, in fact she was horrified. Luckily the wine tasted nice and the meal passed off well. My going away hat for the evening had been made from a cornflakes' box and I had covered it in white material and placed a small piece of netting on the top like a pill box hat. Dad had booked a country cottage in Somerset but when we arrived it was a shock. You virtually needed a hacksaw to chop the weeds down to get to the front door'.

Max listened intently, smiling as the story unfolded.

'An acrid smell filled the air when we opened the door. In fact it made me feel like I wanted to vomit. A disgusting stench filled the whole cottage. It was cold, damp and empty. There was no television, no radio and no telephone. The place was bare.

One small two seated sofa was in the lounge and as we ventured around the house we realised there was an attic and a cellar but not much else apart from a double bed. There was nowhere to hang any clothes and the place was creepy. I just wanted to sit down and cry. I urged dad to take me back home. He apologised but insisted we stay. I hated it.

That evening dad suggested we go to the cinema and we ended up seeing the Exorcist. I was beside myself with fright and entering the cottage at the end of the evening was a major trauma for me. I wrapped cold sheets around my body and I can recall just staring into the air for ages trying to get to sleep.

As usual, dad was snoring in seconds. Because I was keeping my eyes wide open I was startled when the door of the bedroom started to move, creaking as it slowly opened. Then, wham! it flew open. I screamed loudly and gouged my false nails into dad's chest. He leapt up out of the bed, bellowing too.'

Max giggled.

'There's someone in the house,' I cried. 'You have to go and look around. There is definitely someone here. The door rammed open.

Dad looked concerned and crept around the cottage. I insisted that he go into the cellar and the attic. I was petrified, and despite him not finding anything to worry about I stayed awake all night. I was so upset that we left the next day and went home to the flat we were renting.'

Max chuckled.

'Typical dad. Bet he got it cheap?'

'Yes of course Max. His sister said it was a nice place and she could get a deal but I think the deal was a haunted house for a fiver.'

Max laughed as he clambered down into the hull questioning Gordon about what time we were leaving. I followed, getting my lifejacket on ready for our departure.

We headed down the Cowes River and made our way to Hamble for lunch. Sunny skies warmed our faces and we all seemed in good spirits. We treated Gordon to lunch and I enjoyed a couple of small glasses of wine. The men drank beer. We had a mezze, chicken salad, curry and lasagne.

Afterwards we proceeded with another lesson about when to use flares, what colour to use at night and during the day and we went over helicopter rescues, weather, tidal streams and heights, life rafts and navigation skills.

Pulling out the sails, we headed towards Sykes marina for the evening. People sat on the veranda of the marina bar and watched our arrival. I hated everyone staring, willing us to make a big hash of mooring up.

Some children hollered as they threw a ball backwards and forwards. When the ball came over the balcony and landed on the boat, Max picked it up and threw it back to more screams of delight. This was our last night. We settled down to dinner in the restaurant, sank a few drinks and laughed loudly.

When we woke up we all had a bit of a thick head. A few groans here and there rattled through the hull. Today we were heading back to Brighton and the weather seemed perfect for sailing.

Alex cooked a full English breakfast which seemed to settle our hangovers for the final leg of our journey. A long sail lay before us and I was glad that this was our final day.

Seagulls swooped, chattering as they flew ahead of us as we motored out to sea. A good steady wind meant we were able to sail all the way back to Brighton. A northerly breeze was ideal for us. There was not much wave but we managed a reasonable speed. Our sail back went without a hitch and on arriving Gordon asked me to reverse Water Baby into her berth.

'Oh hell,' I thought. 'I have never reversed her into a mooring'. I shut my eyes briefly and prayed that it went well.

I took the helm and as we went past the mooring I revved her in reverse, ready to back in. The wind blew and I seemed to misjudge it. I could see I was going to crash into another boat.

I burst into tears and completely lost it, screaming for Alex to take over from me. A big bang confirmed I'd hit it. I ran away from the helm and Alex jumped in to take control.

Without a doubt, I knew I had failed and I cried even more. Everyone was running around grabbing fenders to use as a buffer and I just stood and snivelled. Alex moored her and I felt intensely angry. I was so cross with myself and I just ripped off my lifejacket and stormed off towards the ladies' toilets.

Inside the toilet I sobbed, not caring that some people were confused and watching me, obviously wondering what on earth was wrong with me. I felt humiliated and embarrassed at my final finish. It was a shambles and Lord knows what Gordon must be thinking.

Eventually I calmed down and sheepishly came out of the toilet. I didn't want to return to the boat but realised I couldn't hide in the loo forever. As I made my way back to the boat, I felt ashamed. Gordon ignored what had happened but I decided to talk to him about it.

'I am so sorry it all went pear shaped. I tried hard, really I did. It just seemed as if the wind blew and I went off course. Plus I lacked confidence, that's for sure.' I wanted some sort of reassurance but Gordon just said, 'Don't worry. Experience will help in the future.'

He walked away.

After stowing away the lifejackets and navigation equipment we were allocated chores in order to clean Water Baby up. Max scrubbed the fridge out and Alex tidied up the ropes. I had to refill the water tanks and then scrub the decks and remove all the sea salt from the boat. Gordon then said it was time to sit down and discuss our previous five days.

My eyes were still swollen from my fit of crying and as I nestled into the lounge seat I felt vulnerable. Everyone huddled up in close proximity. Gordon said we had all passed and I burst into tears again. I couldn't believe I had qualified, especially after my disastrous reversing. I sat open mouthed with tears rolling down my cheeks.

'Alana, you have to have more confidence. Reversing is difficult but you can't go abandoning the wheel and shouting for Alex. The more practice you get the better you will be able to reverse, but remember that as time goes by you will improve. Tears won't change things but determination to do well will.'

Gordon nodded towards me. I could have put my arms around him and given him a squeeze but I restrained myself. One thing I have to admit is that the reversing accident had knocked my confidence a great deal. A mixture of feelings raced through me. One minute I was elated, but I was annoyed and nervous too.

I was proud of Max and Alex. They had done exceptionally well and their expertise in all they had achieved made me feel slightly jealous. Joe, our other son, would have told me that being jealous is not very nice. I know this but I did feel jealous. I had found everything so complicated and difficult when it was clearly easy for the men.

MEN'S NAUTICAL NAUGHTINESS

Back home we had a full week at work and when the weekend came round Alex wanted to go sailing.

I was in the passenger seat on the drive to Brighton and I watched the wind blowing all the trees.

'It's very windy Alex. It seems as if there is a little bit too much wind to go out today?' I knew he'd get cross.

'For Pete's sake Alana, stop going on. It will be fine. Just stop being ridiculous.'

I sat quietly and tears pricked my eyes. I was nervous and worried about the conditions we would find when we set out.

After doing all the engine checks and clipping our lifejackets on, we headed out to sea. Large waves jostled the water on exit and the boat rolled from side to side. Immediately I begged Alex for us to go back but he told me to stop worrying and continued through the high swell.

'I want to go back in Alex,' I was crying again.

I was being thrown about the boat like a rolling ball. It panicked me.

I started shouting, 'Take me in you silly sod. Are you trying to kill me?'

I bellowed so loudly you could have heard me on the moon.

Alex's face looked demonic as he turned the boat round and we returned to the marina. Silence filled the air; Alex chose not to talk to me.

Silence got the better of him and he couldn't stay quiet any longer.

He hissed at me, 'We've bought this boat and you are so bloody useless that were not going to be able to use it.'

It was incredibly awkward and the next few days at home were quiet. It was making me feel ill with worry.

Over the next few weekends sailing had been a mixed bag. On calmer days I was fine but when the sea was choppy I struggled to settle. On another rough day at sea when Robert came out with us he told me for the second time that I should never have bought a boat if I couldn't cope with rough weather. I was most indignant and thought he was a cheeky bugger for saying that to me. In fact I wanted to tell him to fuck off but I bit my tongue.

Unfortunately it was true. I was struggling. As Alex and Robert dropped me off at the visitor's pontoon again and sailed back out to sea, I felt an overwhelming sense of sadness rip through me. I was losing my husband to the boat. I had wanted to buy the boat so we could do something together instead of watching sport every weekend but now my idea had backfired and sailing was taking over Alex's life. For months I'd tried to be part of this, to get better, but it had been a horrendous effort and still continued to be week after week. My dreams of champagne days were just a distant thought.

I wandered to the boardwalk, sat outside in the wind and ordered a large glass of white wine. In fact I had two!

'They're not so clever either,' I thought when I remembered the time they went out on Robert's smaller boat. Sailing far too close in shore outside the marina wall, they had had problems with the spinnaker. As the spinnaker dropped it fell into the sea. Alex ran the boat over the spinnaker and the propeller chewed it up. As he was trying to release the spinnaker his life jacket inflated. A right couple of Charlie's!

About an hour later Alex telephoned to say they were back in, so I supped my wine and went to meet them.

They were enjoying a couple of beers so I opened a bottle of wine and poured a large glass. Chilling on deck, I thought aloud and announced, 'I am going to get a facelift when I am 50.'

Alex retorted, 'Why don't you get them to sew your lips up at the same time.'

Robert laughed, 'Funny, very funny.'

I squirmed back, pulling a strange face.

'Oh shut up. You men don't know how lucky you are. At least you don't have to face a real menopause.'

'Well we do have to put up with twenty erections a day,' Alex giggled. I gasped. Surprised to hear they get up to twenty a day.

I asked, 'Do they happen for no reason?'

Smirking, he replied, 'I don't know but next time I will look down and ask it.'

The tension which had filled the air dispersed and we continued to have a laugh.

Another boat was attempting to moor up and they too made a big hash of it. Then I said something very silly considering my recent reversing accident.

'Why is he so stressed?' I asked Alex as this poor man negotiated the pontoon.

'You'd be stressed if you had a penis growing out of your forehead.'

Robert and Alex hooted with laughter. Man jokes filled the air.

'Don't mind me,' I thought, as the jokes got dirtier.

Alex had consumed a few beers and they were talking about girls liking big men. Alex decided to announce that in his old age he had trebled in thickness down there and girls would definitely be impressed.

'If I laid by a pool, the girls would drool', he enthused. No wonder his nose is growing!

'Oh please, that's disgusting. Behave yourselves. Are you looking in the same mirror as me?'

I shook my head. I assumed this was the sort of banter that men come out with on a night out.

'Hang on a minute. What did you think I am talking about? I'm telling you about my belly,' he shrilled, getting up slowly and patting his tum.

Shortly afterwards Alex went down to the heads for a wee. On his return he came upstairs with the toilet seat round his neck like a big polo mint. He was laughing his head off.

Robert boomed, 'I'm going to get my wanger out and piss on his head.'

'What on earth are you doing?'

I was amused but shocked to see the seat over his head like a necklace.

'It broke at sea today, Robert gave it some welly and his big fat arse wobbled and cranked it off the hinges.'

He continued to wear the toilet seat as if it was some sort of trophy.

Laughter had finished off the day well and everyone departed in a flurry of giggles.

A good spate of warm weather had been forecast and Alex decided we were going to sail down to the Solent. Part of me was excited but the other part was petrified. I knew the next few days ahead were forecast to be relatively calm, so if it stayed settled we would be fine, but on the other hand, if the wind got up we could be in bother again.

Setting off, all was well. The sun shone beautifully and the blue skies were splattered with small puffs of cloud. Alex put some '70s disco music on and I jigged about as we sailed swiftly along.

Calm seas were a welcome sight and to be honest, the whole journey was brilliant. I had no reason to get in a state and I really enjoyed the fine sail to Yarmouth. It took us about twelve hours.

Alex did most of the sailing and often we put her on auto pilot. It was late when we arrived so a meal of pasta and sauce plus a few glasses of wine set us up nicely for bed.

When we woke we found that another boat had moored herself onto our portside. This meant strangers clambering over our boat. Unable to moor onto a land pontoon, we had to get a water taxi to take us to the harbour master to pay for the mooring.

Radioing ahead, we asked for a water taxi to come and assist us. As the taxi pulled up alongside us, I sat down on the wooden pontoon and eased myself towards the boat. As he pulled closer I dragged my backside along the pontoon and let out the most enormous scream.

'Oh my arse! My arse! My arse!'

I fell forwards in the small boat, grabbing my bum.

'What's wrong?' Alex frowned.

'Oh shit, shit, shit. I've hurt my arse Alex,' I said, straightening up and wobbling while trying to stand. I lifted the cheek part of my shorts up on both sides and slightly bent over.

'Look at it for me please.' I begged.

He bent down to have a nose, embarrassed that the taxi man was waiting for us. In fact I had part of my bum hanging out whilst stood on his boat.

'Oh blimey Alana! Your arse is absolutely covered in big splinters. I mean really big ones, loads of them. Yuck.'

I knew I'd hurt myself. My backside was badly stinging. I explained to the man I was going to have to get out and sort my bum out and we'd call him again later. His smile said it all. I expect he went back to his work mates and had a damn good giggle at my expense.

Getting back out of the taxi, I crawled on my knees, trying hard not to get splinters in them either. Alex held my hands and helped me up. Back on our boat Alex was poised with my eyebrow tweezers and a torch. I lay flat on the bed with my knickers down round my ankles and he proceeded to shine the torch on the offending fragments sticking out of my bum. Gently, he tried to pull them out. Despite the pain I couldn't stop giggling. It was not soft giggles but big, grinding, ear piercing guffaws. It had been such a long time since I'd laughed so hard that my tummy was hurting.

I then heard footsteps and the people from the boat next door were walking over ours to get to theirs. I rolled over on my side and looked up. Two children were peering through our cabin window. I started to laugh even harder, tears of fun rolled from the corners of my eyes. What would they say to their parents?

Alex was sniggering too. I didn't get up but Alex pulled the blind across. Laughing, he had problems steadying his hand to carry on plucking the bits out of my lily white flesh. Snorting with laughter, I wondered what the neighbours must be thinking, and now, when I think back to that incident, I don't think I have ever laughed so much in all my life.

After about an hour Alex thought he had got all of the shards out and we emerged to get the water taxi again. Two stern looking adults gave us a dirty look as we surfaced from below. I decided to apologise for the racket and I started to explain to them what had happened.

The dad appeared to be embarrassed and just mumbled something under his breath. The mother just said OK and as we walked away Alex asked me why I had told them what had happened and I replied, 'Why not?'

Our second attempt at the taxi went much better and we managed to get to the land without any more hitches. Paying for our mooring was easy in the end but Alex wanted to find a pub with real ale and because we had to weave down the lanes, it took us ages to find the right place.

Before getting the taxi back to the boat I wanted to use the toilet so I went to reception and asked for the code for the locked door. Outside the toilet I entered the code but it didn't work. I tried again, again and again.

When I went back into the reception I said that I was having trouble getting into the toilet.

'No that's fool proof,' he smiled. 'Go and try again.'

So off I went and repeated the action. Still it wouldn't open. I went back in.

'Look I'm no fool but it's not opening.'

The man asked me to follow him out. We ventured along only to find I had been trying to get into the laundry room.

'OK, I am a fool. I admit it and I have definitely been trying the wrong door.'

He winked at me and let me into the toilet.

Afterwards I went back into the reception and they were all pulling my leg.

'No fool like an old fool,' they joked.

Cheeky buggers I thought.

I am not averse to getting into funny situations and it made me think about my sister Kacie and me when we went down the pub recently.

Our local pub was quiet and as we entered there were two other men sitting at another table just across the way from us. Kacie and I get on so well and were engrossed in our chatter. I whispered to Kacie that I needed to fart and she said that she had a good idea.

'I'll tell you what we will do,' she said. 'I will start coughing and as I cough really loud, you let it go and hopefully no one will hear it.'

So Kacie leant towards me and started coughing but before I could let one go she farted loudly and it sounded very bad. The two men's heads whizzed round knowing, full well she had farted. We both started to hoot with laughter and so did the men. It was giggle time as she sported a big red, mortified face and even apologised to them. Classic!

On another occasion, while on holiday in Greece we were sitting in a bar with our husbands. I looked up and noticed Kacie was not at the table anymore. I asked her hubby where she had gone.

He replied that he thought she had gone to the toilet. Ages passed and she had not returned, so off I went to find her.

'Kacie, Kacie are you in here?' my voice echoed.

'Oh luvvy. Thank God you've come,' she boomed.

'I've shit myself,' she said with desperation in her voice.

'Oh you dirty devil. What do you want me to do?'

'Can you wash my costume out for me in the sink, please? I'm sorry to ask sweetheart but I've got no other option,' she pleaded.

How can you say no to someone, especially if she is your sister? I was supposedly enjoying a relaxing holiday but I had moved from the sun to gagging and I was trying hard to wash the costume out before someone else came in.

Ten minutes later we returned to the table after scrubbing with tons of soap and Kacie was back in her costume. It was as clean as I could get it and she went off to change. The things we do for the people we love! I hoped that she appreciated it and to this day I pull her leg over it, often saying, 'Do you remember the day you shit yourself?' Sisters!

Yarmouth was a quaint place and our visit had been memorable.

Returning back to Brighton again we were lucky that the weather was warm and the winds were favourable.

Our sail back was uneventful, even peaceful. My confidence grew.

Several months later, I had started working as an outreach worker, driving a big bus which toured local villages offering help and supporting families with any difficulties they might be experiencing.

The weather had changed and the winds grew stronger. The Saturday after Christmas came and Alex suggested we go sailing. I'd heard the wind howling down our chimney and the trees were not just swaying but bending.

'It's too windy. Look at the trees.'

My eyes darted to each window in our lounge, watching the movement of every tree, bush and the swinging Christmas lights. Their ferocity confirmed it was hellish outside.

'I'm not going sailing today. It would be terrible.' I moaned.

'Don't be so ridiculous. How can you tell from the trees? It may not be windy at the marina.'

'Well I am not going. It looks too dangerous. I am not coming with you.'

I could feel my heart beating faster and I was getting into a state.

'Why the hell don't you just stop being so stupid and get yourself ready and come?' he peered at me. I just couldn't bring myself to go. I felt sorry for Alex as it must be so frustrating for him but I just seemed to panic and go cold with numbness. I was petrified. Not his fault but me bottling the situation. I had to get away. I just ran off.

Running into the bedroom I grabbed some clothes and left the house. I was in a terrible shape and cried as I drove away. I didn't know where I was going but headed towards Gatwick Airport. It was Saturday morning and at East Grinstead the local library was open.

Pushing past a queue of people trying to borrow books, I raced towards reception to see if I could go on one of their computers for half an hour. I searched the internet for late hotel bookings. I carried my bag into a hotel which appeared quite quirky. Dark thick wooden planks lined the corridor wall. They were quite oppressive and made me feel even bleaker.

I entered my room. It was dispiriting and sitting on the edge of the bed I cried. It was creepy. I felt so unloved and lonely. My determination at all I strived to do was waning. Challenges were just that, but this sailing lark had been unbearable at times. I had been going from loving it to hating it. The traumas of the last year or so had impacted on my moods and my coping mechanisms. I was struggling to keep it together. I think I was very down. Poor Alex must have wondered what on earth was going on in my head?

I turned the TV on and snuggled under the bed clothes. I felt empty in soul and wondered why someone who tries so hard is always treated with disrespect.

I telephoned Kacie and told her where I was and we chatted for about forty five minutes. Kacie was kind and perked me up enough to persuade me to go and find some food. Once again I was perched in a restaurant on my own, this time, eating fajitas and sipping a large glass of wine.

People stared at me. I ate quickly and returned to my room and went to bed.

On Monday morning I needed to go into work. My manager was glancing at me most of the morning and after lunch she called me in to her office.

'Take a seat Alana. Is everything OK?'

I burst into tears, blabbering out what had happened and that I was residing at a nearby hotel. She swung into support mode, telling me she thought I was not in the right frame of mind to be at work. She sent me back to the hotel, reassuring me she would keep in touch.

A few days later I returned to work and on my first day back my manager asked me to come into her office as she had something to tell me. She proceeded to divulge to me she had told her manager about my situation. I was livid. How dare she breach my confidentiality when she hadn't even discussed it with me before opening her big mouth.

As days went by I hated her and a few weeks down the line I handed my notice in. I could never trust her or work with that interfering woman again.

Since her unprofessional handling of my circumstances, I had driven home that day. Settling in back at our house I was determined to try to keep sailing but knew my emotions and ability were not always gifted in that direction. As weeks went by Alex usually went out to sea with Robert in the rougher weather and I'd stay at home in the warmth and safety of our four walls.

One afternoon, after sailing with Robert, Alex revealed they were considering doing the Royal Escape Race from Brighton to Fécamp in France.

'Do you want to come?'

'Oh it's a right laugh,' I thought. I'd bought the boat thinking closeness and champagne but all I'd got was grief, challenges, a lot of unhappiness and a husband who wanted to bugger off on a weekend with his single mate who used to be married to my friend.

'I don't know, I'll think about it,' I replied curtly.

Petrified at the thought of sailing sixty four nautical miles taking about fifteen hours or so, my heart sunk to the lowest I had ever felt.

So many questions ran through my brain: 'What if we sink at sea? What if there is a storm? What if I get seasick? What if we crash into a big tanker in the main channel shipping lane? What choices did I have? I could stay at home and mope or take the bull by the horns and say yes.'

Seventy five boats jostled for a good position at the beginning of the race. I was keeping a thorough look out. Robert had paid for four t shirts in dark green with' Water Baby Crew' printed on the back. We all had them on. Josh, Robert's son was with us.

Tension grew as boats weaved within yards of each other. Waves lapped on the bow as we ploughed near the starting buoy. Chatter filled the air. Voices bounced from vessel to vessel, some with anger at each other for sailing too close and nearly colliding. It was bizarre. I couldn't believe I was perched on the seat waiting for the horn to sound the start of the race. Was I really stupid? Will it all end in tears?

Someone crossed our bow and cut right across us. Alex turned away, nearly hitting the other boat, smacking straight into the big yellow buoy which was supposed to signify the starting line. We thought we would be disqualified for hitting it but as far as we knew we had not been penalised.

As we sailed back round to the correct starting position the horn sounded. We nudged for space.

I screamed, 'Everyone's in the same boat,' I thought about what I'd said and then added, 'but they're not are they.'

It was a weird observation. There was mayhem on the sea. Footsteps hammered across Water Baby and our eyes shot glances in all directions while we all paid attention to the approaching yachts. Battling yachts surrounded us but as we continued several miles out to sea. The boats seemed to drift apart and make their own long way towards the finishing line.

Luckily the weather was kind to us. The waves were of medium height and the sun shone brightly. It was quite exciting and soon we were laughing and mucking about at sea.

Our journey had taken about three hours so far and boredom was starting to creep in. I cracked open a bottle of wine and the guys had a couple of lagers.

'I know, let's play a game,' said Josh.

Josh is twenty two and sports a big luscious mop of curly dark hair which he often runs his fingers through. His green eyes regularly twinkle with mischief.

'What sort of game?' we all enquired.

'I've got a great game. It's called, if I had a vagina. It's a real laugh,' he stated.

I expect he could see my surprised face but proceeded to tell everyone how to play it. Being the only woman on the boat, I was flabbergasted. Firstly, I was in a bloody race that had filled me with fear to take part in and now I was going to play 'If I had a vagina'.

So, bobbing along mid channel in the direction of France, we began to play a game which was going to have me sinking in my seat.

'If I had a vagina, I would put an Aardvark in it,' Josh grinned.

'If I had a vagina I would put an Aardvark and a bull in it,' Robert tittered.

'If I had a vagina, I'd put an Aardvark, a bull and a cow in It,' cackled Alex.

It seemed unreasonable when it was my turn because I do have a vagina and would never get an aardvark, bull or cow anywhere near it and yet it was now my turn. Feeling ridiculous, I said, 'If I had a vagina, I would put an Aardvark, bull, cow and a dick in it.'

I shrilled with laughter and the men roared too. Once we got into the game it was funny and despite the awkwardness I'd felt at the beginning, it did get hilarious, trying to remember what we were fitting into the cavernous body part.

I had naughtily downed a whole bottle of wine. Exhaustion came over me and I announced that I was going to lie down.

My head hit the pillow, the wine calmed me and I fell asleep trusting my fellow crew and the captain to get us to France.

About an hour later I awoke and popped my head up on deck. Josh had made some sandwiches. Soon we would be approaching the shipping lanes.

'Oh Alex! You've sat in your sandwich and it is stuck to your butt,' I said as I creased up.

Alex whinged that I had put it there and it wasn't very funny.

'I've been asleep you silly idiot,' I bemused.

Alex peeled the sandwich off his backside as the men laughed at him. He loathed that.

He carried on eating his squashed sandwich alongside squeals of disgust from us all. The males called him a dirty pig as he scoffed it in.

Imminently, the shipping lanes loomed in the distance. Large tankers, container ships and bulk carriers steamed across our bow. Our passage became harrowing. We had to slip in between the ships, ensuring that we were not chopped in half by these colossal vessels as they continued their voyage.

All of us were willing our boat to keep a steady speed. We did not want the wind to change in pace or direction as this could prove fatal. Tense emotions eased as we safely negotiated the crossing. Our mood lifted and laughter rang around the boat. There was a real sense of triumph as the lane petered out behind us into the expanse of the briny.

A beautiful sunset captivated us all. It was a deep red streaked together with horizontal clouds zipping across the sky before us. I captured some stunning photographs as the sun descended, disappearing down into the horizon.

Our sails were luffing and flapping gently. There was no wind. It had given up the ghost and died. Land was within sight and it was so frustrating flopping about at sea, going nowhere fast.

It was about 9 o'clock at night. We had not seen many yachts as we had journeyed across the channel but we observed a couple of silhouettes of sails in the darkness some distance away. Lights from the land shone in the remoteness, beckoning us to finish the race.

With no wind and the tide going against us we were beginning to get frantic. We were making no headway at all. Rules meant that putting the engine on would go against us but after floating for an hour that is what we had to do.

We safely arrived in France at 10.40pm, position 16th out of 20 in our class. Thankfully we were not last.

We inched our way into the harbour as a few people stood on a wall shouting and waving, welcoming us in. Waving back, it was great to know we were a few minutes from land and would soon be popping our champagne to celebrate.

It wasn't easy to negotiate our track in the dark. We felt disorientated but eventually we saw a free mooring and decided to tie up there, even if it wasn't the right place.

Pop! The cork shot up in the air. Four plastic flute glasses were filled to the brim with the fizzing chilled champers. Ecstatic to have finished, each and every one of us had massive grins and as we chinked our glasses there was a great sense of satisfaction.

Bags of assorted crisps and peanuts helped to deal with our pangs of hunger. It had been such an exciting day but the sea air and concentration took its toll. We all rolled into our beds.

Next morning the sun was shining and it felt odd being in France. Robert had got up earlier and been to the bakery to buy some French sticks for breakfast. We ripped lumps off the bread and enjoyed some ham and a selection of mature cheeses.

Today's schedule would be interesting as this morning it was free celebration drinks and a buffet and then this afternoon, the presentation of cups for the winners and a prize for the loser too. Tonight a big party was planned in a hotel for all skippers and crew.

By about 11.30am I had downed several glasses of orange juice and champagne. The men had been supping numerous different beers.

Giggles, laughter and excitement filled the air as the presentation grew closer. Whooping, clapping and piss taking were the order of the afternoon, as one after the other skippers collected their prizes. Sadly we were not recognised with a cup for our achievements but it had to be said, being proud of ourselves was more than enough of a booster.

Loud disco music blared out, Drink was flowing freely and some really funny dancing was taking place. People rolled onto the floor. A shop who had sponsored the race had given out big goody bags. These sacks had been ripped up and people were wearing them over their bodies like dresses. Drinks were getting spilt and some hard flirting was going on within some groups of people.

Josh was looking the worse for wear and Robert confided that he was considering carrying him back to our boat. I had only had a couple of dances and although I'd been drinking most of the day I was relatively sober.

It was quite funny watching the antics in the room. I wondered how some of them would be able to sail back to

England in the morning; I knew some had scheduled to depart.

It was clear that we would stay in France another day as the forecast meant that it was too windy for us to return the following day.

In the morning Josh looked like something out of a horror movie. His hair resembled a serious electric shock, his face was crumpled and his wrinkled eyes were only half open.

'Hey good looking!' I laughed.

Everyone was laughing at the state of him and when we had all gathered ourselves we sauntered along to watch some of the braver sailors set off back to Brighton. We were shocked that some were returning in such strong winds. It was quite remarkable. Eight foot plus waves battered their bows as they left the safety of the harbour behind. We found out later that many of them had been violently seasick. Mad, absolutely mad!

Meandering through the small streets in Fécamp, we stumbled across a shop that would deliver wine to our boat.

We bought two cases of dry French wine and when we went back to our boat it was neatly stacked in the cockpit.

As the sun went down, we ambled on a long walk, ending up in a very classy French restaurant overlooking the harbour. It was a beautiful setting but unfortunately the food didn't live up to expectations. No compliments to the chef on this occasion!

Waking up early, we returned to England. I had spent a lot of yesterday with thoughts of impending disaster. Watching those boats returning the day before had quite frightened me and although I knew we had arrived in France safely, the journey home was seriously worrying me. I tried hard to keep my thoughts to myself and not outwardly verbalise them. It was almost certain that if I did, I would have been called names and my concerns would have just been laughed at.

Luckily the weather was calmer and the forecast seemed similar to when we had sailed across, but that could change at any time.

After all the safety checks had been completed we set sail. Alex was reassuring me that, although the waves were fairly rough, they would calm down as they were a residue from the powerful white caps yesterday.

Soul music blared from our vessel and Robert moaned that he hated Alex's choice of songs. He preferred rock music which I hated. I would rather die at sea than have to listen to that for twelve hours.

Alex realised he had received a missed call on his phone and it was from the nursing home where his mother was.

'Oh dear, have they left a message?' I asked.

Last time we'd had a call his mum had broken her hip.

'I hope it's not serious,' I exclaimed.

Alex tried several times to connect to voicemail but as we were out in the channel it appeared he had no signal. Getting agitated, he continued to try to access his voicemails but an hour later he still hadn't been able to connect.

'It's ringing.'

I could see he was absorbed trying to hear what the message said. Robert, Josh and I waited with baited breath to hear what was wrong.

'Would you bloody believe it?' Alex yelled

'What, what's wrong?' I demanded.

'Well would you credit it? It has taken me one and a half hours and about £3.50 to find out my mother is constipated.'

I clasped my hand over my mouth trying to stop the laughter coming out but I needn't have worried. Robert and Josh made up for that and the rest of the way home, Alex took a ribbing.

I can remember when I was about fourteen and in hospital having my bunions removed and bed bound, telling the nurse I was constipated. She had made me sit on a bed pan for ages and just as I was successfully managing to go there was a knock on the window behind me. I jolted round to see my boyfriend at the time peering through the pane of glass. I was horrified and didn't live that down for a long time. I had no idea he had been standing there watching me.

France disappeared as if it had never existed. Some yachts were visible as we sailed back to Brighton. Four foot waves lashed the bow. Huddled together in the cockpit, we chatted to pass the time away.

Robert is a tallish chap with a slim build. His hair is balding at the back. He has a kind nature and is always willing to help although in the past his comments have really pissed me off. It's funny though, sometimes Alex and Robert clash over sailing techniques or what's the best solution. I always say what I think but often it is ignored. I often sit back and watch the love hate relationship unfold before me.

Unfortunately, the wind had again dropped right off so we had to motor for quite a lot of the way back. Our adventure home was without any problems whatsoever. I was thrilled when we tied up and our feet hit the welcoming pontoons of the marina.

Managing to have the courage to go to France and returning too was a major step forward for me and I was so chuffed that I was smiling for days and boasting a bit.

CALAMITIES ROUND THE WORLD

Summer was approaching and Alex was determined we were going to take six weeks off work and sail through the warm season.

'We will sail to the West Country and take it in bite size chunks,' he beamed.

I had stocked the boat to the brim and although I was once again enthusiastic, my nerves were on edge. Cornwall was such a long way to go and so many weeks apart from my gorgeous boys.

I had bought about thirty toilet rolls and had made a tower of them in the bathroom at home. It had raised a few chuckles.

'Mum what on earth is that? Max grinned, pointing at the loo rolls.

Smiling back, I said it was my way of looking after them. So an Eifel Tower of toilet rolls, freezers stacked full, fridges bulging and cupboards stocked. The house could take no more provisions.

As I headed for the boat I felt sad. I really didn't want to leave Joe and Max to fend for themselves.

When setting off the next morning, the conditions were good. Our first stop would be Chichester. As the days went by we made our way along the South Coast until we sailed past the Needles, just off the Isle of Wight.

That day was rough. We had to be very careful sailing as there were rocks on one side and shallow shingle ledges on the other, which could be very dangerous.

I couldn't settle and was very tense as we sailed towards Poole in Dorset. I was willing us to get to our destination without problems and when we arrived I was overwhelmed with relief. For the next five days we encountered 50 mile an hour winds and were bound to stay put.

It was incredibly boring and an elderly sailor from a boat across the way decided to come and talk to me. His conversations started pleasantly enough. Then he frightened the life out of me by telling me that on the next leg of our trip were the races where he and his wife had nearly died at sea.

His wife was shouting, 'We are going to die,' as they heaped over incredible waves, the boat listing from side to side. With every wave twisting and turning them, they believed it was their lot.

'You need to know what you are doing to go through the races. I've been sailing for years but honestly thought we were goners.'

I felt as numb as an ice cube. I shivered.

'That must have been terrifying!' I gestured to him.

His grey ruffled beard drooped as his bottom lip confirmed the horror they had encountered. I can't describe the fear I felt, other than to say I had made up my mind that Poole was as far as I was going. To make the next leg of our trip filled me with so much dread that I felt physically sick.

Alex was watching a film on the computer when I went back down into the hull. He was engrossed so I decided to wait to tell him that I'd reached the end of the road on our trip.

Eventually Alex shut the computer and I knew that when I told him my decision there would be ructions.

'Alex, I don't want to carry on anymore. I've just been talking to an elderly sailor and he has frightened the life out of me. I don't want to go through the races. He and his wife nearly died going through them,' I appealed.

'Bloody hell, Alana! Don't be ridiculous.'

He looked shocked.

'I am not going on anymore Alex. I want to go home.'

Alex was fuming, I couldn't blame him though. I picked up my hand bag and left the boat, I needed to think. Walking along, I became quite alarmed as it was getting dark and I was in a strange place.

Dark capped Community Support Officers were moseying towards me. I stopped and asked them if they could direct me to a hotel. I was crapping myself as I walked past a dark tunnel and a man dressed in dark clothing lumbered towards me.

I could feel panic welling up inside me. I ran to cross the road, avoiding his path, my feet padding violently along the street. Finally, I arrived at the hotel but they told me they were fully booked. Once again, my footsteps pounded the floor. This time, reflecting my mood.

I decided to head back to the boat as at least I knew I could sleep there. Alex gave me filthy looks on my return and intermittently shouted at me, asking me what on earth he was going to do.

I knew it wasn't the best situation to be in but I had one hundred per cent made my mind up that this journey was over for me.

'Maybe Robert could come and help you?' I urged. Alex shook his head, fed up with me.

It wasn't long before Alex had spoken to Robert and he had kindly agreed to sail Water Baby back with him. My sister's husband was on his way to collect me from Poole and drive me home. I was relieved. Alex had his mate arriving and I would be going home to the safety and comfort of my own home and I was looking forward to seeing my lovely sons.

I cuddled Joe and Max on my return as I tried to explain what had happened. They could tell the situation was not good with their dad having to enlist the help of Robert to sail back. Joe didn't see the fascination with sailing anyway, but Max knew it could be very challenging.

111

I had a few days to myself now and a chance to relax. Laying down on my bed with a face pack on I started reminiscing about some fun and challenging times we'd had on holiday. Every year, ever since our boys were little, without fail we would go with Kacie and her family on holiday. On one holiday I had dry lips and said to Kacie I was going up to my room to get some lip salve, but on my return she was horrified to see half of my lips were hanging off and all peeling very badly.

'Oh you silly cow Alana, what have you done?' She yelled, most concerned.

Instead of lip salve I had Bazukered my lips with Bazuker That Veruca. Having two tubes that looked similar, I had grabbed it from the drawer and, I had applied it thickly, only to be bawling in seconds as it started burning my lips.

By the time I had got to the sink to rinse my lips it was too late. The skin was hanging off and I was reeling with pain. Despite the drama, everyone found it incredibly funny and all holiday, they took the piss out of me for Bazukering my lips.

On a holiday in Spain by the pool; Alex was shouting at another man. He had tried, in his Spanish accent, to lure me to his bedroom. I had been swimming and having a great time jumping up in the air and yelping 'Yahoo'.

I have to admit I was topless at the time. This man had come over and was trying to persuade me to go to his room with him. Dirty little devil!

'Oh no, I don't want to go to your room,' I said, shooing him away.

When Alex saw what was happening he made his way over and started to shout, 'Adios, Adios, Adios,' pointing at the man frantically, then pointing in the air for him to go away.

Adios is goodbye in Spanish. It was amusing to see Alex fighting verbally to keep me safe and away from another man's clutches. It was a rare occurrence of this behaviour but most men won't stand for a predator in their relationship.

Twice on holiday I have been in earthquakes and on such occasions your brain just struggles to try to work out what is going on.

My first earthquake was early in the morning. I was lying in bed awake when the mattress started to shake. My mind was confused, trying to fathom out what was going on.

My initial reaction was that I thought Alex was having a fit. I stared at him but his face was so peaceful that I decided that wasn't what was wrong. Next, I thought that the neighbours must be having a good old sex session. Maybe the banging on the wall was vibrating on our bed.

'Blimey, they're lively!' I thought.

I was still desperately wondering what was happening when I looked at the ceiling and I could see the roof join and wall rocking from side to side.

It was then I screamed, 'Earthquake.'

Alex woke up in a fright. Grabbing my dressing gown, we fled from the room. I ran down the corridor hammering on the doors of the boys' room, hollering desperately for them to get out.

Mustering together on the lawn was quite frightening and the earthquake measured 6.5 on the Richter scale but we all survived.

I recognised the second earthquake straight away. I was lying on the bed after a hefty dinner. My belly was bulging as if I had eaten an elephant and suddenly my relaxing rest ended in a full blown sprint down eight flights of stairs.

Rushing past, I saw someone pushing someone in a wheel chair and to this day I feel so guilty I didn't stop to help them. Not that I could have lifted the chair, but of course they were unable to use the lifts and I had run on, trying to save my own life. I saw them later they were Ok.

I remember the breaking of glass all around me as I was running, the ground vibrating hard and plaster coming off the walls. Outside I just wanted to go home. Greece had lost its appeal for the second time!

I was dreading Alex getting back from Poole because he was angry that I had abandoned our six week sailing trip. I felt terrible about leaving the passage but when it doesn't feel right, it's best to be honest. I was a mess with worry. On his return things were uncomfortable, he had taken a lot of time off work. I so wished I'd had more courage and not felt so frightened.

Alex seemed obsessed with sailing and that is all that mattered in his world at this point.

Gradually, as time went by, the fact I came home began to fade away. Our next plan was to sail in the Caribbean. It sounded adventurous but an incredibly expensive option. We spent several hours talking about the trip and whether it was a good idea. I had raised a lot of concerns. Alex reminded me that I couldn't just get someone else to take over the sailing of the boat and I'd have a long way to go to get home if I bottled it.

I spoke to the holiday company Sunsail, asking them to tell me more about the weather and sailing conditions. I was assured that the sea was fairly steady with up to 25 knots of wind each day. Good sailing but not too hairy! My mind seemed to be at peace with going and I really was keen to go.

We hired a 36ft yacht which was part of a flotilla. We flew with Virgin Airways to Antigua, continuing on to Tortola. At Antigua we were welcomed with a cool drink and a gyrating man in a pink suit, singing his heart out with Caribbean songs. It helped pass the time as we queued to go through passport control, security and then come back to check in with the next airline.

Looking through the plane window as we circled the British Virgin Islands I thought that the views were stunning. Dazzling, glistening blue seas stretched as far as the eye could see. There were scattered islands with white sandy beaches arching in the distance. It felt like I was watching a movie.

My ears were hurting with the noise from the aircraft, a twin propeller plane. The vibrations went through my whole body. A deep whirring filled my ears and I couldn't wait to land and get off the contraption. There was such a massive difference between the up to date jumbo we flew out on in the first part of our journey.

After disembarking, we waited in long queues, concerned that our transfer would be waiting for us. Outside, a clapped out old flat-bed truck with ripped seats awaited our arrival. We clambered on board, our knees squashed against the pew in front. We were loaded up with like-minded people.

The engine roared into action and we clattered along the streets and struggled up the hills. Willing the wagon to make it up the inclines, everyone was laughing. At times it was jaw dropping being inches away from sheer drops, which led down the cliffs and then directly into the sea.

Finally we arrived. I was glad to get my feet firmly on the ground. You could hear the sighs of relief as everyone jumped off. Our luggage was coming separately in another van. In fact the luggage had travelled in comfort and style in a mini bus whereas we were jostled, jiggled and bumped about in a vehicle that would have been condemned in the UK.

On arrival we were given a full briefing about all the boat's features. Our shopping, which included cold wine and beer, should have already been stocked. We had ordered the food on the internet back home in England and hey presto; it was already put away in the cupboards and fridge.

It was very late at night and after unpacking our clothes, we cuddled up, falling fast into a slumber.

Next morning we received our scheduled briefing which was great fun. Our skipper on the lead boat was Dutch. He was a tall thin young man with a wicked sense of humour. Our engineer was called Lyndsay. Twelve other boats were part of our flotilla. Dutch and Lyndsay were going to look after us. We hoped we wouldn't need Lindsey's help as that would mean there was something wrong with the boat.

Surrounded by palm trees, every morning we attended a briefing to discuss our sailing destination for the day and to receive a weather forecast.

There were quite a few characters on the flotilla and one particular woman was a man eater. She flirted like there was no tomorrow and flaunted her bikini clad body, draping it across the bow of her boat at every opportunity. As their boat arrived, she would stand, arms stretched like a star, so the men could admire her form, always looking around to see who was watching her. I learnt to despise her. It was like a bad egg arriving at each destination. I watched Alex waiting for her to stare at him. When she finally glanced, he did a belly flop into the sea. I secretly giggled as his big plop was supposed to scream, 'Look at me. I am a peacock'.

Every other night a group meal took place. I hated them. One woman talked incessantly and an elderly man decided to hand out toothpicks. Everyone proceeded to drag out bits of food from their gnashers. It turned my stomach. I thought I would throw up. Whoever invented toothpicks is disgusting. It's the worst, most revolting invention ever.

One couple we became friendly with had agreed that, once back in England, we should meet for a sail on Water Baby.

Sailing along in the streaming sunlight, Alex and I had been relaxing whilst the autopilot steered the boat. Seeing land drawing nearer, we decided to take the autopilot off but it was stuck fast. No matter what we both did we were unable to release it. Panic set in as we headed for land and had no control over the boat. Our steering was locked on a firm setting heading towards jagged rocks.

Tugging, pulling, pushing and lots of huffing and puffing, did not free us from the doom of disaster. Radioing ahead to the lead boat, we relayed that we were on a crash course. Lyndsay gave Alex advice over the radio to try different ways of fixing the autopilot but they all failed. Eventually Alex launched himself at the wheel banging the autopilot with all his might. With a big clang, the autopilot fell off and rolled into the sea. We now had steering and were ecstatic, but as the machinery bit the dust, it rolled along the deck and it was now sinking to the bottom of the ocean. How was Alex going to explain that it had flown off the boat and out to sea.

Lyndsay knew the autopilot had been dodgy as we had struggled with it on a few other occasions, but this had been a near disaster.

Unable to leave the bay until Lyndsay had returned with a new part, we chilled out drinking rum and coke. A fit of drunken giggles sounded out. We'd had far too much to drink.

Dutch arrived in his tender. He held onto the side of the yacht and spoke, trying several times to give us the rest of the day's schedule but the two of us kept laughing for no reason. In the end he gave up, pointed to a bar and said 'See you there about 6pm'.

I bet he was glad to leave the edge of the boat because we just couldn't seem to stop laughing at absolutely nothing.

I scoured the sea every day for a sighting of dolphins but I was disappointed. Not once did I see one of those beautiful creatures. A couple of turtles popped their heads above the gentle waves and looked around but on seeing our boat they dipped quickly back into the water. Dustbin lid sized jelly fish also floated by. They were amazing to watch and orange and black in colour. In fact they tricked me into thinking they were turtle shells at first, but on closer inspection they were not solid.

Our holiday was magical. The blue crystal seas, warm sunshine and Caribbean hospitality had been great fun. Our group meals were a chore and I wished there had been less of them. Sitting with people you probably wouldn't choose to if you had a choice, I found annoying at times.

Arriving back in England I was pleased to be home. Alex had arranged for us to go sailing with our friends Charlotte and Richard. Our plan was to sail for a couple of hours and then to go for a late lunch.

Rough seas slapped the boat, but not so rough that we couldn't pop open the rose champagne. Pink fizz tickled our taste buds and some fresh sushi went down a real treat. Breezing up, the wind gusted making the sail a little bumpier, so we all agreed we'd had enough and we headed towards the marina.

Charlotte and Richard's sailing ability was limited. They sat tight in their seats while I went along the boat setting up the fenders for our mooring. I had mentioned the extent of the wind earlier to Alex and raised concerns at how we were going to get the boat in safely.

I moved on to the step fender halfway down the side of the boat and got ready to jump off with the stern rope as Alex reversed in. Alex misjudged the berthing. To avoid hitting the catamaran on our starboard side he put the boat into forward and then the wind blew hard in a gust and I could see I was going to be in trouble. I tried to move my leg but within seconds it was trapped between our boat and the anchor on the neighbouring boat.

I began screaming, my leg was entombed by tons of heavy steel and our boat. The sheer weight of our boat was pushing my leg further into the solid rusty anchor.

Charlotte began screaming, 'Alana! Your leg! It's bending in the other direction.'

I honestly thought I was going to lose my leg.

Alex seemed to be oblivious to the fact that I was being crushed. I couldn't move my leg. It was completely trapped. Luckily it was the flat part of the anchor squashing my leg because if it had been the pointed part it would have ripped my leg off.

It seemed like ages before I was able to release my leg. The wind eased and Alex seemed to gain some control of the boat. I threw a rope to a man shouting on the pontoon.

I rolled in agony. I had no feeling in my foot, toes or leg.

Alex was shocked when he realised I had been hurt so badly. He called an ambulance whilst peering down at my pitiful state.

I lay on the deck but the sun shone so hard onto my shocked body that I was feeling sick. My thigh was black as blood oozed to the surface of the skin.

Charlotte went down below and bought a pillow up to lay over my face so I was in the shade. Pain surged through the whole leg and I could hardly move.

About fifteen minutes passed before the paramedic arrived. He introduced himself as Steve. He asked me lots of questions which I answered as best as I could but I was unable to use my leg at all. I had to hop on my good leg.

Ten stone of me lay on a board and was lowered slowly onto the trolley which was promptly wheeled to the ambulance. With every bump I could have bawled. The paramedics were trying to encourage me to take gas and air but as I was feeling sick, I didn't think the combination of alcohol with gas and air would mix. I'd only had two small glasses and certainly hadn't felt tipsy, but it had affected my judgement.

Whoever invented speed bumps is stupid. It bloody kills a damaged human body when an ambulance drives over the humps. The paramedics discussed cancelling the air ambulance which had been called.

Steve offered his expert opinion.

'I think you've probably broken your leg.'

The other paramedic, whose name I didn't catch, said he thought I had too. I knew the pain was unbearable. Under my knee, something else had dug in so deeply that it was like a cone of skin down to the bone and a very odd shape.

While I was being pushed along the corridor a woman ran past with a head wound with blood pouring down her face.

A nurse offered me codeine for the pain while pulling the curtains around me in the A & E department

I explained I'd consumed two glasses of wine but she felt it would be OK. I also needed a wee so getting me on a bed pan was a feat in itself. I was so pleased that I had another leg which I could use to take all my weight. Very unglamorously, I plonked on the bed pan. I was in agony.

A gorgeous doctor examined me.

'I think we need to x-ray your hip, lower leg and your thigh area,' he said, sternly staring at the whole limb. It took hours to get the x-rays done.

'Mrs Cowell.'

I was expecting the worst as the paramedics had seemed to be keen to give me their verdict.

'You are very lucky. There are no signs of any breaks in the leg or thigh.'

He smoothed his hair back.

'You are badly bruised and a severe crushing of the muscles has taken place. This means you may experience internal bleeding, but if this happens your urine will turn black or show blood over the next few days.'

He placed the paperwork on my bed, leaning towards me.

'That sounds terrible. Could I die?' I whined in pain.

'No, you won't die but just be aware of the risks. Come back if you are worried at all.'

I was given crutches and taken on to a short stay ward for a little while.

Annoyingly, I needed the bed pan again. This time it was a different nurse. She was huffing and puffing as much as to say everything was too much. Why she was a nurse I have no idea. She was so impatient and bad tempered that she should have been ashamed to say that she cared for patients, because she didn't! If anything, she made me very apprehensive and uncomfortable.

After a couple of hours a doctor came in and asked me to try to get up because he had going home in mind.

I slowly got up from the bed but the pain was so excruciating that I immediately felt very ill. My hands and arms were tingling and the doctor made me sit down and took my blood pressure. It had dropped very low. My heart was racing and bumping as if it was going to come out of my chest.

'Try and eat something,' the doctor encouraged, but I said I was feeling so sick that eating was not an option.

They gave me some more painkillers and hoped that in half an hour I could attempt to get up again.

Eventually I managed to get up and go home. I was unsteady on the crutches and was so pleased when I finally got through the door.

For the next five days I was in agony. I was unable to put my foot to the ground and my leg was so swollen it felt like it would burst. Dark bruising flowed down the whole leg and severe grazing was across the complete thigh. The dent below the knee had swollen out of all proportion and the leg became distorted. On day six I was able to put my leg to the ground but it still needed the support of the crutches. I was so bored and I had become a permanent feature on the sofa.

Beautiful sunny days had dominated the last week. Alex had not been sailing but another race to France was organised for the coming weekend. I knew I was not going to make it.

Max and his girlfriend had taken time off work to take part in the race so it wasn't an option to cancel it.

Saying goodbye was difficult. I knew I would be home alone for at least five days. Alex had stocked the fridge with fresh veg and meat for dinners. It seemed so quiet on my own and I was nervous about sleeping in the house alone; it was something I had not done for ages.

The Royal Escape Race went well and they came eighteenth out of twenty four. I had received a text to say they had arrived about midnight. It was a long day as they had woken up at 5am to get ready to leave at 6am to be at the line for 7am. Unfortunately the lack of wind meant it took them until 8am to cross the starting line.

Kacie, and a couple of my friends, were coming over. We went down to the local pub and sat outside. It was a lovely evening and we had a good laugh but when I got home and the door closed, I felt abandoned and alone and I hated it. I kept some lights on all night and the TV playing in my bedroom. I hardly slept. Night after night I hated the loneliness.

After five days they returned from France and I was really pleased to see them all. They brought back six bottles of French wine and they were gratefully received.

Five weeks later I was still out of action. The muscle was red, swollen and very painful to touch. Luckily I was feeling much better than I had been but unfortunately I was now very nervous about getting back on the boat. However, I could bend my leg and had been swimming a few times to get the strength back into it.

The deliberation about whether to go back on the boat filled me with dread. I had now completely lost my confidence and was petrified. I made it clear that I would only go out on a calm day. I needed to build up the courage it takes to jump between boat and the pontoon whilst mooring. Only then, would I be comfortable leaving the harbour & sailing in rougher conditions.

TARTS, FLASHERS AND NUMBER TWOS

Robert was always turning up with different women to come sailing on our boat.

It was coming up to August and the Airbourne show at Eastbourne was going to be on. Robert wanted to bring another woman who he decided to describe as deck candy. I was really annoyed. Did he think our boat was some dating tool? I did appreciate Robert coming though as it meant I had someone to help jump off the boat to moor up.

War planes were beckoning as we sailed towards Eastbourne. The air show was spectacular.

Robert's woman friend was less than gracious towards me in the evening as we got ready. In fact she was quite a nasty person.

As we were showering, she asked me what I was going to wear. I said it was a casual American restaurant where we were going. I explained that I would be wearing a maxi dress and she agreed and assured me she would go casual too as she didn't want to feel out of place.

On exiting the boat that evening she looked like she was going to a major dinner dance. She wore killer high heels and a tight silk off the shoulder dress. She wiggled her arse like she had a serious dose of Vaseline between her bum cheeks. She exaggerated her walk and she was verbally so over the top towards the men.

Her body language screamed 'I'll shag anyone or anything.' It was embarrassing.

Even at breakfast, when asked why she hadn't eaten much, she gestured that she was a little-and-often girl and continued to make tacky suggestions to my husband and Robert.

I hated having her on the boat. She was tarty and flirtatious which made me feel very uncomfortable, so I left the men to her and got the bus back to Brighton Marina. Luckily Max had come with us too. He decided to leave with me and we ventured to the cinema. He didn't mind accompanying me. I told Alex I wasn't feeling very good and left them to sail back with Miss Tarty in tow.

Superb views of the sea along the white cliffs enabled Max and I to enjoy the bus journey back to Brighton Marina and we followed up the cinema trip with a few drinks at the pub.

About 5.30 we sauntered back to the boat and as we walked along the boardwalk Robert and Mrs I'll Drop my Drawers for Anyone, were walking towards us. I was pleasant enough but glad to see the back of her. An invite back to the boat will never come her way, I emphasised to Max as we continued towards the yacht.

It was several days later when I told Alex how much of a bitch I thought she had been. He didn't understand it but most men are on an ego trip when a woman is purposely throwing her cleavage down their neck.

This week was going to be busy, I would be joining Alex for his weekly visit to his mum and I was working as a counsellor at two local hospitals. Arriving at the nursing home we waved at the usual faces sitting in the lounge area.

Music blared out for their reminiscing session. Smiles filled the room and several people sung along to the old time tunes.

Alex's mum was sitting in her usual chair tucked in the corner of her room. For months now Elizabeth had not wanted to leave the security of her room. On the last occasion that I had wheeled Elizabeth down to the pub, I'd just bought her a drink when she said that she wanted to go back to the home. I didn't even get a chance to drink my glass of wine. She was bellowing that she wanted the toilet and as she needed two members of staff to help her, I had no choice but to return. I'd asked her five minutes before we left if she had needed the loo.

This time we kissed Elizabeth and within minutes of our arrival she was insisting she needed to go to the toilet.

'I think you should call the nursing staff Alex. They will need to help your mum.'

Elizabeth's demanding became a little on the stroppy side.

'I want to go to the toilet and I want to go now'

'Alex, I really do think you should call the nursing staff. It is in your mum's best interests'.

Alex scowled at me.

'If my mum wants to go to the toilet, then she will go to the toilet now,' he scoffed sternly, putting me in my place.

'Your mum should have two nurses to help her for health and safety reasons. If she falls, it will be very dangerous. If you are not prepared to wait, I am sorry but I am not going to help as I think it's a recipe for a disaster.'

I shook my head.

Alex struggled and helped his mum up from the chair and eventually got her into the toilet but within minutes Alex began shouting.

'Mum, Mum, don't do that Mum. Oh Mum, oh no it's all over your hands. Mum stop it's all over your hands.'

There was urgency in his voice.

I have to admit I had started to chuckle as I could hear the commotion, and then it got worse.

'Oh my god mum, it's in your hair. Get your hands down mum. It's in your hair.'

I just couldn't stop silent laughing and I shouted to Alex that I was going to wait in the garden.

I did feel terribly mean but the way he had reprimanded me for not allowing his mother to do what she wanted had backfired on him.

126

As I walked towards the warmth of the sun, I did inform the nursing staff that they were needed and a pair or two of gloves were a definite requirement!

Later that day I had a physiotherapy appointment for my damaged leg. I had been told to use a wobble board to strengthen my leg. It was a circular disc with a bulge at the bottom and the objective was to balance upon it. Concentrating, and wobbling away in the small rehabilitation section, a man came in to use the other equipment.

Saying hello, he proceeded to say that he needed to change but instead of going to the changing rooms, he just dropped his trousers and was completely starker's below his waist.

Immediately I looked down to the floor, not wanting to gaze up again in case I got another eyeful. Fiddling about, he took ages to get his tracksuit bottoms on and I think he was purposely parading his wares in front of me. I swayed off the board and left the room quickly. Finding one of the physiotherapists, I told them they had a flasher in the gym.

'There is some man in there with his willy out,' I whispered through the reception window.

Anne, the physiotherapist, grabbed a walking stick as she emerged from the office door. Lord knows what she was going to do with that!

I decided I was leaving, cutting short my physiotherapy for the day. I wanted to come back the next week so I asked them to make sure they didn't schedule in the flasher at the same time.

'You have a pervert in your midst,' I laughed as I left, waving goodbye.

High pressure was forecast for the weekend and we were looking forward to a good sail. I still hadn't jumped off the boat since my accident so I was feeling very uneasy about the forthcoming sail.

I snuggled up on the Friday night so that I could be ready for an early sail Saturday morning.

I awoke with butterflies in my tummy. Showering down at the services block I suddenly realised I had forgotten my towel but I was sodden. Grabbing a load of toilet paper I started to wipe myself down while reprimanding myself for being so stupid.

Soon I realised that my body was covered in bits of white soft loo roll and I looked as if I'd been in a snow storm. I had no option but to stand, wait for it to dry and then try scraping the tissue off my body.

Several fellow sailors greeted me with a cheery, 'Good morning' as I emerged from the wet and wild shower block.

Tightening up my life jacket, I felt exceptionally neurotic with regard to sailing that day. I had been secretly torturing myself with frightening thoughts about dying at sea, how I nearly lost my leg in the big crush and how it could have been pulled right off, just hanging there attached to the neighbour's anchor like a bit of dead meat.

Learning from my big mistake, I now know to never stand or sit on the edge of a boat when mooring. No more offering the adjacent boat a chance to destroy me.

Giving myself a good inner talking to, I persuaded myself that when I need to jump off the boat my leg will not crumple underneath me or disintegrate. I also knew that I had come this far so thoughts of giving up, although tempting, needed to be batted away.

Today's schedule comprised a sail to the Solent. Friends, Serena and Graham who we had met in the Caribbean, were meeting us at Chichester Harbour.

Fabulous sea conditions beckoned us as we sailed out from Brighton. Flat seas and a strong northerly wind were ideal. As I pulled out the sails I sighed with relief. Keeping at a steady speed of 6 knots, we arrived quicker than expected.

Waving furiously, Serena stood on the pontoon and greeted us with a cheery smile. Glad to see her again, I gestured back. Graham stood with his arms stretched out to take the line from me. I was comforted as once again I didn't need to jump off the boat. Psychologically this had become an intense problem for me. My mind seemed to be fixated on the negative perception of me hurting myself again, not being able to walk and crashing the boat or denting someone else's boat.

In fact two years prior to this accident I'd suffered a serious fall in a skiing accident. I tore both the lateral ligaments and the cruciate ligament in my knee and fractured the lower part of the same leg that the anchor had crushed. I had to be taken by skidoo to a waiting ambulance, my useless leg dangling to the side.

'We must operate,' the doctor said.

I'd bottled out of the operation, instead opting to come back to England for treatment. As the insurance company had refused to pay for Alex to stay and look after me, I didn't want to have to stay on my own in Austria while recovering. Going back to the UK would be more beneficial.

My insurance company paid for three seats aboard the plane for my leg to be outstretched on the flight. I was carried everywhere in a wheelchair while at the airport. Back home the hospital consultant said that as I was not very sporty he didn't have to operate and the scar tissue would heal in twelve weeks. In the meantime I scuttled about in a wheelchair.

While willing the fracture and ligaments to heal, I embarked on a lonely three months stuck at home before I could start going out on my own again. After tons of physiotherapy, and thankfully no flashers, I began to make good progress.

'Come for an evening,' I'd offered Serena and Graham, but three days later they were still on board. They were a lovely couple but they were definitely outstaying their welcome.

Fog engulfed the sea. A harsh wind was blowing and many boats took to the shelter of the port. A drenched skipper moored alongside us. He told us that he had been sailing for most of his life but said that his sail that day had been the worst he had ever experienced. He relayed that going out today would be pretty mindless and quite treacherous so we stayed another day, unable to get Serena and Graham to their car.

Sitting in a local Chinese restaurant, a beautifully manicured silk gowned waitress attended to our every need. A waiter hovered near the next table to us while we drank a few beers and some fantastic tasting wine. Several times he had tried to take the food order but had been sent away by a rough looking and hard spoken man; he was quite rude to him. The waiter was dark suited, tall and quite imposing.

Walking over for about the third time, he stood at the man's table and said in a strong Chinese accent, 'wha' you wan' ass-hole?'

I felt my eyes widen and I darted a look towards Alex. He eyeballed me and we both started to giggle. I asked Alex what he'd heard. He confirmed what I thought he'd said.

Our guests had not overheard but when we tried to explain what had happened they explained how they had been completely oblivious.

So, next time you go into a Chinese restaurant behave yourself or you could suffer the 'arsehole' treatment. I believe the guy deserved it. He made himself look ludicrous and he was totally unaware he'd been named and shamed.

While leaving the restaurant my phone rang. One of my old school friends had just had a boob job, an uplift where they take the nipple off and reposition it further up the breast. She was recovering well,

A few months back we'd sat discussing the forthcoming procedure. Laughing hysterically I spluttered, 'Make sure they don't keep the window open or when they remove your nipple, a peckish bird could fly in and grab it for a snack. Then you'd have to have a teat from a baby's bottle sewn on.'

Much hilarity filled the air and we confirmed that we knew plenty of men who needed their dick relocating to their forehead. Glad to hear her nipples were in the right place, I said my goodbyes until I could find time to visit her in hospital.

Walking back to the boat we found that the weather had closed in even further so it looked like it would be a cosy chat huddled in the hull for us.

Graham, a small statured man, was retired now but he used to be a diplomat abroad. Serena had been a ballet dancer. Her tiny frame assisted in her working all over the world. I'm afraid my jobs were far from as glamorous as their lives.

Embarrassingly, I only had tales to tell of much lesser significance, such as the time I worked in a pub thirty years ago. There was a fire blazing in the middle of the room and it was decorated in an old fashioned style. The landlord was fantastic. If we worked hard then we'd be rewarded.

I worked alongside another lady called Renee. We always had a fantastic laugh. Our incentives for working like troopers came in the form of a lovely big bonus at Christmas, hampers from Body shop and once we were even treated to a day at a health farm. He leant us his flashy car and as we ripped through the countryside we felt on top of the world. Neither of us had dared to visit such a plush place before.

I was a little over eighteen. We did feel a little intimidated. The building was beautifully decorated with chandeliers, crisp white tablecloths and restaurant places set for five course meals.

We opted to rest outside for our lunch using the loungers on the veranda. A long row of recliners spread along the terrace, quite closely positioned next to each other. Each one had a perfectly pampered dressing gowned human laying on it. I think we were trying to fit in and act all posh when, without warning, I proceeded to fart really loudly but not on purpose - it just popped out. Renee' had just taken a sip of her tea when she caught her breath. Gasping with shock, she started to choke violently, so much so that she vomited to the side of her sunbed and I eventually fell off mine laughing.

It just seemed so inappropriate to let out a big toot but I had no control over my bum that afternoon. It just crept out. Furthermore, it was disgraceful behaviour from Renee to actually be sick in such luxurious surroundings. So many posh accented people were glaring at us and therefore the giggling took over and it became a riot of naughtiness with both of us spending the rest of the day's experience chuckling incessantly. We were very pleased and surprised not to be asked to leave.

When I look back, if I'd have done that today I would have been mortified. Oh what it is to be young, disrespectful and naïve.

One particular incident thirty years ago still leaves me feeling very ashamed. At the time I thought it was hilarious.

My boss had been really unfair towards us. I honestly cannot remember what he did but for a laugh, and to get our own back, we decided to put fart powder in his tea. Mixing up the concoction, I was really worried he might notice it while he was drinking. It went down a treat and then we waited for the farting.

Secretly giggling and huddling together, we watched from a distance as he started to rub his tummy but instead of just farting he spent the rest of the day in the toilet with an upset stomach. Oh Renee' and I did feel really bad as it was only supposed to be a joke but unfortunately it went a bit wrong. Neither of us confessed to him and we are still in touch all these years later. I would be so ashamed if he ever found out. I feel incredibly guilty as he was the best boss ever. I put it down to being young and not thinking of the possible consequences.

As we get older, most of us definitely become more responsible and behave in a more respectable way. While on holiday with Charlotte and Richard, old friends of ours, we were allocated a room next door to them. Our balconies overlooked a wonderful sea view and I was quietly sunning myself. Warmth engulfed me and I relaxed. When I heard their balcony door open. I was going to jump up and shout boo but then I heard the loudest fart ever!

It was quite unpleasant so I shouted out, 'Charming.'

No one replied. I heard the door opening up again and then shut. I thought to myself 'Now who was that? Charlotte or Richard?'

Later on I told Charlotte what I'd encountered.

'Oh we don't do that in front of each other,' she smiled.

No I thought, 'you just fart in front of your mates instead.'

Neither one of them confessed.

My first date with Alex was a romantic walk and on that occasion he passed wind but, as he did, he scraped his heel along the floor to try to disguise it. I heard him and found it funny.

'I heard that you dirty devil.'

Thirty years on we still laugh at his antics back then. Now he sounds like a trumpet several times a day.

Sixteen years ago I used to work at a company selling beers, fine wines and spirits. Every week I would regularly call pubs, clubs, and hotels for their drinks order. One afternoon my boss asked me to sit on reception. Rupert always wore a cravat, tucked into a crisp white shirt, and a waistcoat. Tailored trousers sharply ironed and highly polished black shoes finished his styling. He spoke in a firm posh voice and I believe that he was privately educated.

Bleak plain walls and a steel slatted staircase sat just in front of the small desk where I was seated. A couple of customers had arrived and I had shown them to the warehouse where they could buy a few goods.

I'd just received an ear bashing on the phone from a very disgruntled customer whose order had not arrived. As I replaced the receiver I heard thundering footsteps across the ceiling. They disturbed my thoughts. The rate and impact of the strides sounded serious.

I jerked back in my chair looking up towards the top of the stairs. Rupert came running through the door with his left hand holding his bum cheeks together and the other steadying himself on the hand rail.

He was like an express train, screaming, 'I need the toilet, I need the toilet. Don't get in my way'.

Half way down the stairs he lost his footing and slid all the way down on his back, landing at the bottom of the stairs. I got out of my chair, crept round the desk and peered at him lying crumpled on the floor.

'Are you OK?'

'No, I've shit myself,' he said most indignantly.

I have never wanted to laugh so much in all my life. My boss was a very well to do man.

I helped him up and it wasn't a pretty sight. I had to keep moving my face to the side, away from his view, to let a cheeky smile out. Poor devil had to drive himself home like that to change. He couldn't exactly call a taxi!

As soon as he left the premises, I ran with bated breath into the sales office and rolled on the floor, laughing so much it hurt.

Everyone doubled up. It was the funniest thing to tell them. They couldn't believe they had missed it. Shitting jokes were the order of the day, every day, for months to come.

Graham and Serena were laughing. Perhaps all these memories are best kept as memories. Recalling them, I have to admit that they are not the most tasteful but they are all true life events.

Blue skies stretched across the sea today and it looked like sailing was an option. Perhaps today Graham and Serena were going to get back to their car. Waves rose to about four feet. It would be a manageable trip but on checking the weather forecast for that day strong winds were predicted for late afternoon.

As much as I had enjoyed their company, it was good to get some private space back. After dropping them off at a harbour near Chichester, we hugged them goodbye.

We had planned to sail back to Brighton that day so we headed towards Selsey Bill. I hated going past Selsey as the waves can get really lethal within minutes.

Knowing the winds were going to be increasing, Alex and I decided to sail out to sea a little to evaluate if we should sail back or not. Further out, although the wind was stronger, Alex persuaded me that he needed to get back to go to work and that we would be fine. I did express my unease but as usual it didn't make any difference. He did what he wanted to do.

WIND WARNING AND A HEARSE

I opened a bottle of wine and poured out a glass, sipping it slowly and using it as a tool for relaxation. I chilled out, hoping that Selsey would be OK.

The sheer power of the water caused the spray to rise into the air, soaking us and the boat. I couldn't believe my eyes as an adult dolphin leapt up through the wave's right by the side of us.

Screaming with pure excitement I leapt off the seat, running towards the guardrail. Imagine a child's Christmas, their most wanted present! That's how it felt. It was exhilarating beyond my wildest dreams.

Three dolphins gave us the show of their lives, leaping high into the air, flipping forwards and backwards, diving under the boat and trailing the surf behind.

I kept on shouting to them how beautiful they were but I am sure they didn't understand me. Hey, who knows? They are so intelligent that maybe they could tell I was happy.

"Turn up the music. They'll love it," I bellowed.

"No, I'm not missing this."

Alex leant right back as one surged up as if it was going to end up laying in the middle of the cockpit. Continuing to sail ahead, we observed a silhouette show for us as we left them behind still dancing on their tails. I yearned to turn the boat back but, as we needed the tide with us, this was not an option.

On my return to Brighton I knew I would register the sightings of the dolphins with Sea Watch, a service which keeps track of observations, and the location, of these beautiful creatures. I grabbed my phone and texted everyone I knew. I couldn't believe I had seen dolphins in the UK when I hadn't seen them once in the Caribbean.

Gradually the wind increased and the waves heaped up. It wasn't long before the bow was crashing and banging through the rollers. A howling wind whipped through the sails and soon we both felt we might need to bring the sails in completely. We had reefed in as much as we could because the boat was heeling over too much, but then the winds started to exceed 34knots. If we didn't act soon the sails could possibly rip.

Despite Water Baby having a good cover hood, the spray was still entering the boat and we were getting cold and wet. An odd feeling of survival took over. Although I was very nervous and frightened, I also knew we had to manage the boat as best we could to try to get back alive.

Maybe the wind would blow even harder? I hoped not. We were several miles out at sea but I could see the gigantic white dome of Butlins at Bognor. Unfortunately I seemed to keep seeing it for several hours. I remembered going there as a child and having such happy times.

We were travelling against the tide and the wind and the conditions were worsening. Having pulled in the sails completely, we were now using the engine. Making headway was so slow. Although turning back was an option, we decided to carry on and get back to Brighton.

'Arrrghhh!' Alex scoffed, sporting a deep frown.

'What's wrong?' I stared intently, catastrophic thoughts filling my brain.

'I don't know what's happened to the fuel gauge. It now says we only have about a quarter of a tank of diesel left.'

He tapped the instrument but the indicator didn't move. I clambered towards him, watching his persistent drumming on the toughened face of glass.

'That's not going to make any difference is it?' I said through gritted teeth.

We were in an immense dilemma. Sailing is not viable and we may not have enough fuel to get back to Brighton. The wind speed intensified to 36 knots, the sea swell slammed into the bow, boom, boom, boom. With every crash the noise was deafening.

'This is serious. If we run out of fuel we are going to have to call the RNLI. How on earth has that happened?' I questioned, holding my face in shock.

We had filled the tank up with diesel a couple of months ago and when we left for this trip we had at least two thirds of a tank of fuel.

'Could we have a fuel leak? The engine can't use that much fuel surely?'

I was panicking and I knew I had to calm down. Getting hysterical would not help matters and we needed to focus on how we could get back safely. But it was beginning to look very worrying.

Thankfully, neither of us was feeling seasick, which was quite incredible under the circumstances. Relentlessly, the waves hit us over and over again as the wind increased further. Having clipped ourselves onto the boat for safety with life lines, we instigated a plan of what we should do if we did run out of fuel.

I get really angry when I think about people relying on the RNLI through their own complete stupidity and I was beginning to think that today we were actually going to join the stupid club. Radioing them would be incredibly embarrassing and I realised that our call for help would also put many innocent men and women at risk. In hindsight, we should never have left Chichester.

In the vast expanse ahead I could begin to see Shoreham chimney, an imposing landmark. This gave me hope because the next port afterwards was Brighton. On the horizon I could see another yacht trying to make way. I felt sorry for their crew too as I knew they must be struggling but I remember thinking. 'I expect they have enough fuel.'

I began fearing the next obstacle. If we managed to get into the marina, how on earth was I going to jump off the boat in such a gale?

Only half the speed of this wind was howling whilst the anchor forced itself into my leg. Could mooring be an impossible task?

Thinking ahead I explained to Alex that I was going to text Robert to see if he was around the marina. I begged him urgently to come and assist us to moor up.

I was relieved when a text flashed up to say he would be there. Shocked to think we were at sea, he understood that we might experience terrible problems trying to get in. I was so eternally grateful that I replied, thanking him with all my heart. On this dreadful occasion we seriously needed him.

I watched the fuel gauge every few minutes. It had gone down even further so we were unsure if we were going to make it. It seemed a never ending journey.

It was so weird knowing there's nothing you can do other than keep going. But when you don't know if you're going to make it, it's so scary.

Aware that the turbulent seas were going to become even more confused at the entrance to the marina, I became gravely concerned. Previously, having watched television footage of RNLI rescues right outside the marina, I knew we were going to battle against the elements and it was not going to be pretty.

Squinting towards the fuel gauge, it appeared we might reach Brighton. Relieved at one blessing, I braced myself for the next real challenge. At this point Water Baby resembled a bucking bronco except on water. She was lurching up and down, listing from side to side. If the keel hadn't existed we'd be over on our side, a knockdown.

Clutching tightly to the table, I tried to steady my whole body. My wet backside was slipping from side to side. My hair was drenched and stuck to my face. I was feeling frozen and exceptionally sorry for us. I wondered if our lives were going to end today.

The wind increased to 38 knots. Shaken like a cocktail, we neared the entrance, tipping up to one side. I was screaming, looking face down at the sea, holding on as tightly as possible.

Alex helmed the boat. Enormous breakers swept towards us and smacked into the marina wall. Skilfully, Alex had to try to steer the boat so that the waves did not hit us purely on the side or we would have definitely suffered.

On our final approach I could see Alex was alarmed as he battled against the elements. Sheer determination and concentration brought us safely into the marina. Straight away I scanned ahead towards the pontoons to catch a glimpse of Robert.

Yes, he was there. Marching up and down the deck I put the fenders out for protection. Still in shock from the terrible arrival, I was taking deep breaths, knowing I had to jump off. Waving frantically, Robert beckoned us towards the visitor's moorings. Continuing on down towards our allocated berth where many other boats reside would not be the most intelligent idea today. Hopefully, the only thing we could smack into here would be the wooden pontoon.

As we got closer, I lobbed a rope to Robert. Luckily he caught it and he pulled her in with all his might until I was close enough to leap off.

'Shit,' I bellowed as I flew through the air and landed safely.

Running fast to the bow of the boat, I tethered her to the cleat, tying it off and taking the sheet back to put a spring on so that she did not move forward. I gave Robert a hug and thanked him profusely. He'd been in the pub with a girlfriend and asked us to join him once we had gathered ourselves.

I recollect catching Alex's eye for a while and although we didn't speak, we held our gaze. We were both acknowledging that we had been tremendously fortunate to arrive in one piece. I was euphoric for having managed to jump off the boat with little pain in my leg. I'd been dreading it so much. I had built the vision up to be a critical barrier to sailing over the last few months.

Delicious smells filled the air as we sauntered into the warm atmosphere of the pub. Steaming over to the open fire, I slid into the most fabulous soft luxurious sofa and huddled into a cosy cushion. My ordeal was over.

Sadly, a few weeks later Alex's mum died. Taking steroids for her arthritis had resulted in the disintegration of her jaw bone. The poison built up in her body and eventually took her.

All her life she'd loved and adored Alex so much. This was going to be a shocking loss to Alex and I was worried how he would cope over the next few months. We had a superb hotel so we booked a meal there for after the funeral for everyone.

I cuddled Alex and made sure he felt loved. Telling Alex his mum was in heaven with his dad and my father, had made it all seem a little more bearable. We had a recording of Alex's dad singing one of his mum's favourite songs. We played it at the end of the service. It was beautiful.

Despondency filled the air. Sorting out Alex's parents' home to be sold was heart breaking but we needed to pay the nursing home fees. I peeked at the chair where Alex's dad used to sit when he played dominos with the children.

He'd lean forward towards them and they'd sit cross legged on the floor.

Granddad would laugh loudly when they tried to cheat and he'd say, 'Now, now then. Behave.'

Their smiling faces reflected the happiness they encountered when being with him. He even taught them to play poker and gamble with pennies. I'd never felt quite comfortable with the gambling side but it was harmless fun and luckily neither of them have ever had a gambling problem.

Folding up all of Elizabeth's clothes affected me badly. Tears gently rolled down my reddened cheeks. I sat on the bed with their possessions, photographs and memorabilia sprawled around me and I cried. Venturing into the garage we spent about four hours stripping it clear and putting most of the rusty tools into a skip.

Traveling along the road going home, I saw something out of the corner of my eye. Making its way across my ski jacket, over my chest was a bulky, jet black spider, I started stamping my feet hard, pounding my upper body like there was no tomorrow, screaming for Alex to stop the car. I nearly had us killed. I was so vocal. I'd frightened Alex enough that he actually swerved the car off the road.

Hysterical, I threw open the door and I jumped out from the passenger seat and started to leap up and down, bashing my body all over with flat palms and rubbing my hair vigorously until it was similar to a bird's nest.

Anyone passing in their car might have thought a freaky scarecrow had come to life, it was that bad. Continuing to wallop myself all over, yelling as if I was being murdered, I needed to know if the spider had gone. Inside the car was a boot full of junk and rubbish. I am certain it came creeping up from there. I demanded that Alex get out of the car and check me over from top to bottom to ensure the spider was not sitting on my back.

We spent quite a while inspecting my seating area in case the spider or any other little shits were lurking. Glad to get home, I fell into my bed, hoping my spider encounters had long gone.

Next morning, I was standing in the post office where I'd queued for ages. Sensing the irritability of most folks, I swallowed hard, trying to supress my tetchy mood as I was next in line. A very elderly lady in front of me shuffled towards the counter.

'Hello dear,' she muttered.

'Good morning Madam. How can I help you,' enquired the middle aged man behind the booth.

'I'd like to apply for a passport renewal for my husband please.'

Leaning on the edge holding her white hair, she peered at him.

Tilting towards her he said, 'Is he over eighteen?'

I couldn't believe my ears. Did he honestly ask an eighty year plus lady if her husband was over eighteen?

Without warning she chastised him.

'How ridiculous! What a silly question to ask a lady of my age. Do you think I am married to a child?'

Glances between the customers waiting became apparent and I just started sniggering.

'Silly sod,' I whispered to the lady standing next to me. Raising her eyebrows she agreed.

Honestly how hair brained? Now he was definitely a smart man, who clearly would do well on his appraisal. He looked sheepish and apologised, trying to make lame excuses for his mistake.

Blunders can be either funny or quite dangerous at times.

Years ago when the boys were small, my mum occasionally cared for them after school. Preparing the dinner one night, she produced a feast of chicken nuggets

144

and chips with baked beans. Seating the children up at the table she positioned the plates in front of them.

'Oh nan, this looks nice,' Max chirped up.

Joe scrutinised his plate.

'Err nan, I think you've cooked my Boilies which I use for fishing. We can't eat them or we'll die.'

My mum ran over to the table.

'What, what have I done?'

Joe explained that she had taken his bait for river fishing from the freezer. Mum cleared the plates really quickly, much to the amusement of the boys.

Twenty years on they still remind nanny that she's a dangerous cook and how she had tried to kill them.

Thankfully, as I moved forward to be served in the post office, the idiot who thought an eighty odd year old possibly had a child for a hubby did not serve me.

Tonight Charlotte was throwing a party as a celebration for her husband's birthday. Luckily she'd been able to buy some expensive fireworks. The food was going to be pretty basic: sausages, jacket potatoes, soup and burgers.

'How do you make mulled wine?' she enquired a few days before.

'I know it's got brandy in it,' I chuckled. 'Pour loads of that in and we'll have a great time.'

Wrapping up well, we braved the dark cold evening air. They'd lit an enormous log fire. Gathering around the flames and warmth felt very snug. Chatter sounded out and later on laughter and shrills of delight tinged the atmosphere.

Crowding together we watched the wonderful fireworks zoom into the air and explode in a shower of beauty.

Charlotte had continuously filled our glasses with mulled wine, which was delicious and very moreish. Back around the fire, I sat on a log and Charlotte joined me.

Giggling, chatting, gossiping and generally telling stories I was heavily into revealing all to Charlotte about an encounter I'd had once. I seemed to be chatting for ages without a response from her, even though she was sat at my side or that's what I thought. On turning my head towards Charlotte, all I found were her legs sticking up in the air. She'd fallen backwards off the log in a drunken stupor and was lying on her back in a big bundle of dead leaves. I gawped directly at her. She had a sly smile on her stoned face.

'Oh, what the hell are you doing, down there?' I grinned.

Cutely she chuckled and although her lips were moving her words didn't make any sense. She was well and truly gone. Clambering off the log, I called several of the men over to help me get her up. Being very fit she didn't weigh very much but as her body was uncontrollable, it was slightly more difficult than we thought. In the end, one of the men flung her over their shoulder and carried her in. She hasn't drunk mulled wine since and following her log incident she felt quite poorly for several days.

It's funny when drinking gets out of hand. We were spending the evening at Kacie's house. She is quite partial to her wine. We were sat at the table. She had cooked a superb meal of prawn curry and a gorgeous caramel pudding. She lives in Hove and many people comment on what a posh area it is.

Huddled on her sofa later that evening, we drank some liqueurs. Kacie's behaviour started to get slightly unpredictable. Her voice echoed loudly as she became more vocal. Her husband was trying to get her to quieten down but the more he requested this, the more she misbehaved and the brasher she became.

It was getting late. Alex was driving so as we said our goodbyes, Kacie stood on her door step.

'Love you Kacie.' I hugged her, 'Thanks for the wonderful meal tonight.'

'That's OK, I love you too,' she shrilled loudly out to the whole street.

It was like her own personal challenge to see how showy she could be, her mission for everyone to hear her, even if they were inside their house. She repeatedly screamed. Alex and I made our way to the car in front of the house and got in, opening the car windows.

Their house is on a tall slant, so her front doorstep is like a stage looking out on the street. Tom was none too pleased. We heard him asking her to come in but she continued to shout. His next ploy really did backfire. He was trying to explain that in this area people didn't behave like that and she was to come back inside the house and quieten down.

Still on the door step, she started lifting her legs up one at a time, swinging them from side to side as if she was doing a slow Can Can. Every time she swung a leg, she also swung her arm high into the air and proceeded to bellow, 'Bloody area.' Lifting her leg to the left, 'Bloody area.' Swinging the other to the right.

Suddenly Tom got her round the neck and dragged her in backwards and slammed the front door. Alex and I were laughing and just about to pull away when the door flew back open and she was at it again. Tom then left her on the step, banging the door shut.

'I can't leave her there, Alex,' I sniggered.

'Silly moo,' I thought.

Easing out of the car, I wandered back up to her. Several of the neighbours were peering out of their doors to see what the commotion was. Calling through the letter box, I asked him to open the front door as I squeezed past her kicking legs.

'Behave yourself Kacie. Come on, you have to be good. Alex wants to go home.'

Kacie seemed to react well to my request and settled down as I led her back into her house.

Plonking her onto the sofa, I told her to stay there and thankfully she did. Waving as I vacated the room, I was really chuffed when she didn't reappear at the entrance again.

In the car returning home I chatted to Alex about Kacie and Colin. They are twins.

'Oh Alex, do you remember the time on April Fools when I phoned my brother Colin up and told him I'd tied you up and you were lying naked on the bed but I couldn't untie the knots?'

Colin had listened on the phone and then there was silence. I'd begged him to come round and help me untie Alex. Colin was none too keen and I said that I would have to cover up his modesty with a blanket. I tried to convince him that I had no idea how the knots had got so tight.

Colin was so relieved when I shouted, 'April Fools.'

Another funny time was a couple of years ago when we received a lovely invite to a meal at our neighbour's house, Andrew and Wendy. Brilliant food adorned the table and another couple of our friends had also been invited, plus Colin and his wife Petula.

I was working as an alcohol counsellor at the time and although I took my role very seriously, on occasion I would have a drink or two and when I was feeling exceptionally naughty, three.

Drink flowing would have been an understatement and Alex was filling his boots.

'Go on Alex, have another brandy.'

Andrew poured another large one into his already half full glass. Sharing the bowls of food, the evening had a really good feel to it but I was beginning to fear that getting Alex home was going to be testing.

Alex was slurring and beaming from ear to ear. Every time he neared the end of his drink they would top it up again. Half a litre of brandy later, I was clenching my teeth. Seeing Alex that drunk was actually not that funny to me. Clearly he was a source of amusement to everyone else but it had been about twenty five years since I had seen him that pissed. I knew he was going to be ill that night and the next day and we were supposed to be going to see my uncle.

Getting up, Alex launched back. Losing his footing and balance, he fell towards the French doors. I managed to prop him up on the back of his shoulders before he smashed through the glass and I was pushing hard to keep him in an upright position. He was staggering all over the place. I held on to him tightly, trying to steer him towards the back door.

Our destination was only across the way but it was a feat in itself trying to get him up the path. If I'd have let go, he'd be rolling face down in the bushes.

Inside the bedroom I bent over slightly trying to take his trousers off. I knew that if I laid him on the bed my lack of strength would not have allowed me to lift him up to get them off.

'Whose legs are they?' Alex bellowed.

I scanned the room with fright.

'Whose legs are those?' he repeated loudly pointing to the mirror.

Confused I glared into the reflection too.

'What on earth are you talking about Alex? They're your legs,' I assured him.

'No. No, come on. I can see someone's legs.'

149

At this point I started laughing.

'You silly sod, they're your legs. No one else's.'

Alex's face softened and he hung onto me with his arms tightly wrapped round my shoulders.

'You don't know how much I love you, do you?' He squeezed me tightly.

'I do sweetheart.'

'No, no you don't realise just how much I love you.'

He lifted his index finger up to his lips, making a 'shhhh' sound and giggled. Unexpectedly he fell back onto the bed, rolled into a ball and within seconds started snoring.

Pulling the covers gently over my hubby, I undressed and cuddled up to him.

Waking in the morning he looked like death. I knew today was going to be a disaster.

Driving towards Bognor to meet my uncle, Alex asked me to stop the car and he promptly threw up on to the side of the road.

Sitting in the restaurant Alex ordered some food but after a couple of mouthfuls he left the rest. My dad died when I was eighteen so seeing my uncle was important to me. I wasn't too happy and quite embarrassed by the state of my husband. Having said that, I know I have humiliated my family on many occasions.

While enjoying a meal in Pizza Express, Joe, my son, and his girlfriend were talking about dares. He'd provoked a friend into stripping off completely naked, running around our garden and then leaping into the pool.

Unfortunately it had been at a family BBQ with elderly relatives, so it didn't go down too well with the aunts in their nineties but I had found it funny.

I've often thought an alternative nursing home with strippers once a week could liven things up.

I think my mates comments were, 'You don't want them having a heart attack!'

Hey ho, I'd rather have a laugh than sit there doing craft.

Joe peered at me across the table.

'I bet you wouldn't stand up and start talking out of your bum like Jim Carey?'

Joe grinned cheekily. I was surprised he had challenged me like that as there are not many things I wouldn't do.

'I am shocked you've asked me to do that Joe. Are you sure?'

I shot a glance at him. The gauntlet was down.

Up I jumped and bent over, clasping my bum cheeks. I pulled them apart, at the same time creating a talking arse. 'Hello Joe, how are you?' I hollered.

'Mum, sit down. For God's sake sit down. Everyone is watching you.'

He seemed to be whispering from the side of his mouth. I stayed leaning forward and repeated my backside chat. I wasn't fazed. I'd not been drinking. After a while I stood up.

Turning round to face Joe, I found that he was as red as a beetroot.

'Sit down,' he hissed.

'Aha, you won't ask me to do that again will you?'

His girlfriend was smiling but never said a word. I wondered if any of her previous boyfriends' mothers had behaved so naughtily.

Just because you're a certain age, it doesn't mean to say you lose your personality and ability to fulfil a dare.

Back home that evening Alex informed me that we needed to service the engine on the boat. Getting a professional in was going to cost a lot of money. Alex is very intelligent so he said he'd try to do it.

'Can I help do it?' I said. I was eager to learn.

Next weekend we had bought all the bits and I started to pump the oil out of the engine. It was a right messy job with oil getting everywhere.

Having succeeded with changing the oil, I was now going to remove the impeller.

'Will a lot of water come out?' I probed.

'There shouldn't be too much,' Alex assured me.

As I undid the screws, water started to leak out from behind the part. Trying to catch the water in a container, I had to keep stopping and pushing the metal plate back as it was flowing too fast. Considerable amounts of water poured out, much more than I'd expected. Eventually the water subsided and I removed the impeller completely, replacing it with a new one.

The filters also needed changing. Although I struggled with them, I finally managed to change all three. It hadn't been easy squashed inside the engine compartment but I felt a real sense of achievement once I had completed the service.

'Let's go and top up with fuel then sweetie. You radio the ahead to the marina and make sure someone is there for us please.'

Alex patted my bottom.

'OK I will.'

Alex was now up on deck turning the engine on and I radioed ahead.

'Brighton Marina, Brighton Marina, Brighton Marina. Water Baby, Water Baby, Water Baby, just asking for someone to attend the fuel pontoon please?'

I waited but there was no reply. I clambered on deck.

'I radioed ahead. They didn't reply but I expect they heard me,' I shouted.

After untying the ropes we headed towards the fuel pontoon. In the distance I could see a person standing on the base. I was so incredibly chuffed with myself. I'd managed to get someone there by using the radio.

After filling her with fuel I went into the cabin to pay. I rummaged in my purse and grabbed my debit card.

'Thanks for coming to help us. I didn't hear anyone reply on the radio so I wasn't sure if anyone would be here or not.'

I smiled gratefully.

'Oh no, I was here anyway. I didn't hear you on the radio.'

The young, long haired man frowned.

As I went back down into the hull to put my purse back in my handbag I looked at the radio. I put my head in my hands and started snorting with laughter I hadn't even turned the radio on, let alone putting it to the correct calling channel.

I decided that after such a positive day I was not going to confess to Alex that I'd not even turned the radio on. Let's face it, why should I? What a dipstick. It would just be laughter fodder for when the men wanted to take the piss out of a woman.

Later that day we set sail for a few hours. Compared to the terrible sea conditions last week it was beautiful and not too choppy. I wouldn't have gone if it had been rough. Last week's battering would last me a lifetime.

All seemed well on deck so I excused myself to go to the toilet. It was fine in the briny so I sat quietly contemplating on the toilet. Within seconds the whole of the loo went pitch black. It really frightened me and I wondered if we were sinking.

I dragged my trousers up and ran up on deck having only half -finished what I'd gone down there for. So what did I see but Alex, very calmly sitting on the window hatch, staring at me and wondering what the commotion was about.

153

I screamed, 'You've sat your arse on the window. I was trying to go to the loo but I was OK one minute and then I couldn't see a thing.'

I poked his tummy.

Alex laughed loudly, poking me back in the ribs. 'Come and cuddle me,' he said, his arm outstretched towards me.

'I need the loo, I didn't quite manage what I went downstairs for, so don't sit on the bloody window you ear hole.' I went back down to the heads. To finish what I had started.

At the end of the day, as we moored, once again I jumped successfully onto the wooden platform and tied her up.

I sat in the sun with a glass of wine, reflecting on a conversation I'd once had with Charlotte. I had been very excited because we were off to a casino with her and Richard.

'We've been to an auction of promises,' Charlotte gleamed.

'I bid on a limousine and we won. In fact I've organised it to take us out this weekend to a posh casino. That's if you can come?'

'Oh yes, that would be lovely. Thanks for asking us. I've never been to a casino before.'

I slipped on a black lace dress and some high heels and spent hours on my makeup, applying Boucheron perfume, some dainty diamante earrings and a fine necklace. Then I glanced at my reflection.

'How thrilling,' I thought,' to be going in a limo.' Rummaging through the coat rack I thought a nice little white imitation fur stole might be the finishing touch. So, slipping it round my shoulders I waited for Charlotte's call to tell me they were outside.

The shrill of the phone sent me into a frenzy of grabbing my clutch bag and pulling my wrap tightly. I tip toed towards our awaiting limo. As I slipped into my seat, for the first few seconds I felt like a film star.

Jabbering with excitement, I started to look around at the interior. Deep, dark, mottled varnished wood surrounded the inside and there were large ornate handles on the door. A musty odour filled my hooter and I began to question what sort of limo it was?

Shit, it gave me the creeps! We were actually in a funeral car, the type which follows the procession. Charlotte was chatting away and I tried to conceal my disgust but my thoughts echoed through my brain constantly. In the end I couldn't hold it in any longer.

'Err Charlotte, I think we are in a hearse thingy. You know the car that follows the coffin? This is not a limo for pleasure.'

She looked at me.

'Yeah I know. We didn't realise that when we bid for it. It was only when it turned up tonight that we gathered it was.'

She looked a little embarrassed. I burst out laughing. It was side splitting after all my excitement and now here I was feeling pretty freaked out. I seriously didn't like it at all and I was pleased on arrival but I was a bit embarrassed when the doorman from the casino opened the door on the car to let me out. I prayed he hadn't noticed it was a funeral car.

Although dreading the return journey, I tried to make the best of the evening. I decided my spend limit would be no more than thirty pounds and within minutes of playing roulette I had won eighty pounds. In my delight I forgot I was in the company of some high browed people and started to do a very energetic celebration dance, waving my hands in a big circle.

Charlotte reprimanded me

'Don't do that here Alana. It's embarrassing,' she hissed.

Told off, I sauntered away. My winnings were safe in my bag and I decided that I was not going to lose my cash.

I wandered around people watching. I sidled up to some chap who was standing on his own and chatted with elation about my win. Then I confessed I'd spine chillingly turned up in a funeral car. He didn't stand talking for long but hot footed it away. I wondered why.

We exited late at night. I skulked in the doorway hoping that when the car pulled up I could jump in quickly so that no one would be conscious that it was a funeral car collecting us.

Scampering in, I slid into my seat and hated every minute of my return journey.

'Good night, thanks,' I said as I waved Charlotte and Richard goodbye. I turned to Alex and said that I hoped that would never happen again and how awful it must have been for them when the car turned up.

Numerous friends either texted or called to see how the limo casino evening had gone and they hooted with laughter when they heard I'd travelled in a funeral car.

IS IT GOODBYE

Water Baby will always have a special place in my heart but as she is a centre cockpit boat, when we are entertaining there is not much room for people and the conditions can be a little squashed.

We deliberated as to whether to buy another boat for some time. Our savings had grown. Alex had previously been made redundant from British Telecom and he'd been given a pay-off to leave.

My experience as a sailor had widened but I was still suffering from being an unhappy seadog at times. I'd achieved my exams but still struggled with navigation. In fact I was still crap at it. I'd been in atrocious conditions at sea, nearly lost my leg, gained hundreds of body bruises and was definitely bewildered that sailing wasn't about drinking champagne. Yet here I was contemplating buying something else. Was I downright stupid?

You only live once Alana, I reminded myself. Don't give up.

As we drove to Port Hamble to view a few boats, I suspected I had finally lost my mind. Going from a thirty six foot boat to a forty foot seemed rather ludicrous. Once again I began imagining what a bigger deck would be like. We could have additional friends on the boat and socialising would be so much easier. On the superior yacht, we could get up to ten seated on deck. On Water Baby, if you only had four people it was squished!

We viewed a Moody yacht. Inside it was beautiful with deep lush furnishings but sadly the cockpit was appalling. There was not enough room to swing a captain's hat, I decided.

Alex appeared to be more bothered about the new boat's sailing capabilities whereas I dreamed of parties on the modern yacht. I'd not had a party as such on Water Baby had I?

No, no parties, just days out sailing or clinging for dear life. As I examined all the 2011 yachts, a surge of enthusiasm raced through me.

Using Alex's phone, we scanned for other boats in the vicinity to go and view. This one was very expensive, in fact far too much. Alex pooh-poohed.

Her name was Serendipity. Knowing that we could possibly afford it if we sold Water Baby, my heart slumped. I'd miss her like a true friend, especially if someone else bought her and I had to watch her being sailed away. This was such a big decision.

When we arrived we were informed that the boat was out of the water on dry land. Gloriously imposing, this Beneteau Oceanis' mast stretched so high into the air that I had to crane my neck to see the top of it.

Ancasta's sales team were on hand to help us board the vessel. Carrying a large telescopic ladder Kevin opened it up bit by bit and lodged it hard into the ground and checked it for stability. He let us to go up the ladder one by one.

I held on tightly. Bouncing up the ladder I went skyward first. The ladder seemed extremely flexible which did not give me a lot of confidence while trying to get on board. Then Alex tailed me. Cocking my leg over, I scaled the safety rail. Smoothing down my outfit I felt quite vulnerable because we were so high up. I grabbed Alex's coat and gave him a tug to help him over.

On deck the room was plentiful and she had two steering wheels, so Alex and I could share being at the helm. I gazed about the cockpit and I could visualise all our friends sitting with drinks, enjoying the sunshine, even if we didn't go out to sail. Downstairs the seating was white leather. It was very plush and it had a microwave, television, two heads, two massive consoles (for GPS and radar), three cabins and the central table lifted down into another double bed, so eight of us could enjoy a bash then conk out in the berths.

It seemed such a lot of money though. I wasn't sure about the interior as Water Baby had sported deep mahogany wood. I gazed around. This reminded me a bit of the inside of a caravan. A lighter wood effect was something I needed to consider. I just wasn't sure.

The salesman was on the case.

'It has a high performance hull and its design means it is elegant with taut lines.'

'Ohhh snazzy,' I laughed. What on earth did that mean? Was he talking about the sails or the main body of the boat?

He explained that the boat had a continuous bilge over the whole length of the boat which gives the hull rigidity for extra safety. He informed us that it had limited heel and would therefore sail much better and closer to the wind than Water Baby.

It had numerous large, lateral windows giving plenty of light. Its features also included a 40HP engine, mainsail area 449 square feet and the genoa 453 square feet, plus a long heavy keel for further stability at sea. Personally, he grabbed my attention when he spoke about all the safety features.

'All means of prevention of dying at sea are vitally important to me,' I winked at him.

She was an absolutely beautiful boat but it just did not grab me like Water Baby had. After I had climbed back down the ladder, I stood back and looked at all the qualities and benefits she offered. I loved the cockpit. She was a grey and white yacht and she looked good. Inside the white leather seats looked chic; there were lots of cabins, a double bed in the lounge area, many safety aspects, better sailing, less heeling and so much more room than my dear Water Baby. Just one negative - the lighter wood effect didn't appear so luxurious.

Alex loved her. The negative for him had been the price. We needed time to think and chew over our options.

So all week we pondered, 'Should we, or shouldn't we?'

'Let's take a break from sailing next weekend Alex, and go to this charity ball I told you about.'

'I'm not sure if I want to go,' he replied screwing up his nose.

'Oh go on, I'll make it worth your while. We can book a hotel room for the night,' I said, winking at him cheekily. A wry smile crossed his lips.

Chugging along the motorway, Alex seemed decidedly calm whilst driving. Normally there was an urgency to get to where he was going. I was pleased he was chilling out for a change. I turned the music up louder when 'Rock Your Baby' by George McCrae came on. It reminded me of when I was a teenager.

Both of us were in good spirits as we entered the opulent hotel. I carried my crimson ball gown over my arm, trying not to let it drag on the floor. I had my overnight bag and didn't waste any time trying to lure Alex into my clutches. I slipped into the bathroom.

'Be out shortly,' I reassured him.

I heard Alex putting the radio on and laying on the bed.

'Great,' I thought. 'Perfect.'

During the week I had secretly gone to Ann Summers and just to spice things up a bit, I had bought a studded neck collar and a whip in black and red. I eased myself into the tight black Basque, suspenders, lace topped stockings and slender black stiletto heels. I wore my lingerie with pride.

160

I felt naughty as I studied my reflection in the mirror.

I finished off with some vibrant red lipstick. As I opened the door Alex had got off the bed and was at the entrance of the room reading a notice plastered to the back of the door. 'Hi,' I whispered, he turned round.

'Oh wow, Oh, look at you,' he drooled.

I lay on the bed waiting for him to come over. I tried to imitate how the movie stars drape themselves sexily across the bed.

With a big grin, Alex speedily ran over towards the bed, launching himself high in the air towards me as if he was on a small trampoline. As he did so, he smacked his head on the ceiling which was low and jutting out. He fell onto the bed, as still as a dodo. He was out like a light.

I jumped up, feeling ridiculously stupid in my collar and wondered if I should call an ambulance. I shook him and patted his face, calling his name over and over again. Gradually he began to stir, groaning and complaining that his head hurt. I tried to reassure him.

I scampered into the bathroom and got a cold flannel and held it over his head. A big red lump appeared on his forehead and it seemed to be growing by the minute.

'Shall I call reception and ask them to get a doctor?' I asked several times over.

'No, I'll be alright but I've got a terrible headache,' he groaned.

'Maybe I should get you to A & E at the local hospital. I can change quickly and we'd be there in ten minutes,' I flustered.

'No, I'll be fine. I just need to be quiet.'

I ran and got my dressing gown on. I wrapped it around me. Reaching to the back of my neck I pulled the studded collar off and threw it on the side.

'You mustn't go to sleep Alex. That's dangerous when you've had a head injury.'

Sitting on the edge of the bed I stayed there for hours, trying to keep him awake. Eventually I fell asleep and when we woke in the morning all our friends pestered us as to why we didn't come downstairs to the ball. I just told them all that Alex had felt unwell. They'd have ribbed him something chronic if they'd known the real reason. I even offered to put some foundation make up on his bump to disguise the evidence.

Back home we had a quiet week, apart from my regular commitments. For well over a year I had been working at an animal rescue centre as a volunteer. Every Tuesday I would get a bottle of water, hat, gloves, a change of clothes, walking boots and a big hug for every dog I walked. I had been doing four hours for a long time but after my anchor accident, I dropped it to three hours.

Smurf was the most fantastic dog, real cutie, and we shared a routine. After collecting him we would spend fifteen minutes in the run playing catch with squeaky toys. Afterwards we had a nice countryside trot for ten minutes and to top it off, a sit down on the bench for doggie treats, cuddles and a gentle massage.

Smurf loved me and I loved him and the day I came back to walk him and found he was gone played havoc with my emotions. I was ecstatic that he had found a home but sad that I wouldn't ever cuddle him again. As I walked past our bench a tear trickled down my cheek. Turning my head away, I felt my heart strings really tug. I knew getting close to the dogs was not the best idea but he'd bowled me over.

I'd videoed Smurf on my phone and when I dropped my phone into a cup of tea, I was devastated that Smurf was no more in my life, other than in my memory.

Working at the centre has had its moments, like the time I was chatting merrily away to a visitor and she was enthralled with the Labradoodle I had on the lead.

Placing her opened handbag on the floor, she proceeded to snuggle into him, stroking his curly frame.

'Oh he's gorgeous. How old is he? Why is he here?'

Both of us were engrossed in our conversation but when I looked down to the side of me, the Labradoodle had cocked his leg and was peeing into her bag.

'Oh crikey, sorry,' I shouted, pulling him away, but it was too late. Her handbag was full of pee.

She pulled everything out onto the floor and seemed none too happy but was willing to accept responsibility that she shouldn't have put her bag on the ground. Her friend was laughing and told her that she'd learn by her mistakes.

Months earlier, making my way indoors to collect the next dog, I handed in the one I had just walked and patiently waited for the next. Chris, one of the permanent workers, started to point at me and laughed.

'Do you realise you're covered in poo? It's all over your back. How the hell did you get that all over you?'

I peered over my shoulder and big brown stains lay right across my back. I had absolutely no idea where the mess had come from but I had thought, whilst walking, that there was a funny smell. Luckily I had a change of coat with me but to this day, how my coat got smeared with poo remains a mystery. My friends occasionally ask if I have seen the phantom shit thrower recently. Thankfully I haven't.

It was Saturday morning and we'd arranged a second viewing on the 40ft Beneteau Oceanis, named Serendipity. We'd discussed changing the boat on and off all week. I was undecided but enthusiastic. I could tell my champagne goggles were looming again - my world of fantasy! I'd go into some sort of dream world forgetting all the bad incidents. It was a bit like giving birth. You forget the trauma. I mustn't give up I thought. I mustn't give up.

Plodding around the deck, I walked along to the bow and lifted up the flap to reveal the anchor. Nestled on the side was the remote control to lower and higher it. I pushed the red button. A grinding noise sounded and I scarpered away.

The boat was such a lot of money but with Alex's redundancy having paid the mortgage we could afford it.

'Let us go for lunch and decide what we want to do.'

Alex grabbed my hand and led me away.

Huddled in the warm yacht club, we ordered our food with a large glass of wine and a beer.

'OK let's buy it. We ought to sell Water Baby as soon as we can. Organising a survey and sea trial will enable us to make up our minds 100%.'

Alex plonked his beer on table and waited for my reply.

I nodded and smiled. So there it was. Decision made.

Ancasta's salesman Jeffery, beamed when we agreed the sale subject to survey. I expect he would gain a nice big commission.

Sitting down in their main showroom, we completed the necessary legal papers. While sipping a hot cup of tea, the receptionist shot several smiles in our direction. Jeffery moved his chair closer to ours and explained that the boat needed to be re-launched for the sea trial and they would have it available for the following weekend.

'Alright brilliant,' we agreed.

'See you next Saturday at 10am.'

Grasping the glossy brochure which accompanied the yacht, I turned the pages over. I couldn't wait to show all my friends, I was so excited and sent out a torrent of texts.

I made some weather enquiries during the week. The forecasts confirmed the sea state would be favourable for the sea assessment. Pleasingly our surveyor had agreed to come out with us to test her thoroughly at sea and complete his job.

She was so much higher than Water Baby now she was in the water and I struggled to climb on board. Jeffery had bought some life jackets and we completed the safety checks before we set off to sea.

Matt, our surveyor, was frantically running around the boat like a rash, lifting up lockers, peering in the engine compartment, checking the seals and seacocks. As a vessel, she felt quite imposing as we advanced along the route we were taking. Gently the yacht bowed forward in the undulating waves. I held on tight to one of the backstays.

Heading towards Southampton, Serendipity was handling well. I was nervous at taking the helm but seemed to manage quite well. I was however, completely surprised when trying to reverse the boat as I didn't seem to have any control over it whatsoever.

I was a little mystified that she appeared to handle no better than Water Baby but Alex swore that she did. I was not convinced. I'd only ever reversed Water Baby three-four times but when I had in the past, it seemed like she was easier to manoeuvre.

Serendipity moved through the water sharply and she categorically sailed much closer to the wind than Water Baby had. Soon we were doing 6 knots and increasing.

I often wondered what an old slide felt like when the children didn't want to play on it any longer. It seemed as if I was dumping Water Baby. I know that this sounds odd. She's just a boat, but to me, she'd lived alongside me during a significant part of my life and sort of supported me through hard times. I oozed affection for her and knew I would be absurdly sad when we parted.

Matt wanted to check the engine and oil pressure, so while underway he let the engine run up to normal operating temperature. He needed to check for any excessive vibration or sound coming from the running mechanisms but to do this he had to vary the speed at which the engine was running, finally bringing the throttle wide open for a couple of minutes.

Serendipity seemed to be performing stylishly and her seaworthiness bowled us over. Thankfully Matt had been able to scrutinise her bottom when she'd been out of the water, inspecting the hull closely for any abnormalities, checking the propeller shaft and hub to blade connection, seeing if the anodes needed replacing, checking for any moisture bubbles and then making sure they applied the anti-foul paint after his once over. We had agreed for the bottom to be painted before she went back in the water or we would have to pay again for her to be lifted out.

Returning to port, Alex walked towards me grinning. We both realised that our new adventure was starting here today.

After finalising all the documents and payments, we arranged to sail Serendipity back from Port Hamble to Brighton. Alex had contacted Robert and his son Josh to see if they could help us navigate her back. It was three weeks until the first available date when we were all able to make the passage. So we had three weeks to wait.

'Let's do a sneaky week sailing in Greece before we collect the boat? I'll look online. We can get a really cheap deal last minute with Sunsail,' I begged Alex.

'There's not enough wind out there Alana. It will be boring.'

'How can sailing in Greece be boring? We can swim off the back of the boat, the weather will be wonderful. Please? We can eat at lovely quaint tavernas and enjoy the food.'

'Ok, you've convinced me. Go and book it then.'

Before we knew it, we had boarded the plane and shared some sweets. Swathed in warm air as we

166

disembarked, we made our way to the 36ft boat we had hired at the Ionian Islands in Greece.

It was the second day into our holiday we were about half an hour from port.

'It's so calm you should start getting the fenders ready now. Also bring back both bow lines then we can just get the stern line off according to where they want us to go.'

Alex had given his orders, so off I went making my way to the bow.

'Oh shit, that hurt! Ow, ow, ow.'

I didn't look down. I'd stood on the bolt for the anchor locker. I was trying to ignore the pain and just carry on through but it didn't work. So I decided to look down to see if I had actually cut my foot. There was blood everywhere including pools of it back along the route I had taken.

I started to shout to Alex that I had hurt myself but he ignored me, clearly thinking I had just had a little accident. This was serious and I was petrified. I shot over to the cockpit, screaming as I flew across.

'No seriously I have hurt myself badly! Get the first aid kit. I am going to bleed to death at sea,' I hollered.

I tried to show Alex but the blood pooled around my foot. I knew I needed to stem the red gore. I threw myself onto my back and raised my leg high. No one was at the helm. Alex was crashing and banging around, down in the hull. Thundering up the steps, he handed me the bright orange box. I grappled at the contents and then, holding a large roll of gauze, I pushed it firmly to the cut. Blood had seeped all the way down my leg, all over my shorts.

'It's like a massacre,' he wailed.

'Call ahead Alex, tell them we need help.'

'Yes it's my wife. She has cut herself badly. I am single handed and she may need to go to hospital if we can't stop the blood.'

I could hear them over the radio saying they were going to send someone out to us on a tender. I was shaking, I was so scared. We were still about 20 minutes off land and they had said there was no hospital on the island. The hostess on the lead boat was trying to find a doctor.

'I think my wife will need stitches. There is blood everywhere.'

I could see that Alex's concerned frown meant he too was wondering what the outcome would be.

'I won't die, will I?'

I was struggling to hold my leg up in the air and stem the blood pouring from my toe. A quick look revealed the middle toe had split right across and the cut was deep. Oozing non-stop blood, I tried pushing harder with the gauze. A tender went past us.

'Is that them?' I huffed.

'No he's gone on.'

'Shout to him. See if he's made a mistake.'

Finally the idiot in the tender came back. Not that he was much use. He just relayed what we had already said back to land.

Alex finally reversed the boat into the mooring they had for us. Several people gathered on deck and stared at me lying on my back.

The skipper from the lead boat was nowhere to be seen. One of the young ladies who were crew off the lead boat boarded.

'I have first aid skills. Let me have a look,' she said and tried to remove the gauze.

'Oh, it's split quite deeply and right across and I can't see why the blood hasn't stopped yet. You've been like that for a while now?'

'I am bleeding badly. Look.'

I pointed to the deck. She grimaced as she observed the blood bath.

'We have tried to locate a doctor for you but there is only one on the island. Unfortunately no one knows where he is. We could take you on another boat ride for about half an hour to the island which does have a hospital. What do you want to do?'

'Does anyone have a stitch kit? Could I stitch it myself?' I shook my head. I didn't want to bleed to death.

'Well let's wait ten minutes to see if the doctor arrives.

'We will ask if anyone has any nursing experience.'

I asked Alex to hold my leg up. I was struggling to keep it elevated. Suddenly this dark haired man sidled up to me.

'I here now. I stop the blood. Yes I stop the blood. Give me foot,' he indicated with his enormous hands.

He continued, 'I ring my son. He come from pharmacy. He bring special medicine to me. Stop blood. We wait.'

I smiled and thanked him, so pleased the doctor had arrived. Relieved I rested my head back on the teak deck.

'My son, he come now. Here see, he come.'

I lifted my head in his direction to see a young man coming down the pontoon with a white bag. Clearly it was from the pharmacy.

My foot was duly grabbed and the doctor started to shake a white powder over my foot and toe. He then started to bind my foot with a bandage. Then I noticed his hands were filthy and his bandaging skills left a lot to be desired! His large dirty hands sported black lined fingernails.

'Oh Christ! Is he really the doctor?' I thought.

He continued wrapping my foot until I balked my eyes at the tightly bound bundle on my foot. A five year old could have done better.

I tugged on the girl's top by her waist.

'Is he the doctor?' I whispered.

'Oh no, he owns the restaurant at the top of the mountain.'

She could see by my eyes that I was not impressed. As much as I thought how kind he had been, I was sure I was now going to die from blood poisoning.

'His hands were filthy. If I put my foot down, it will just pour with blood again,' I whispered from the corner of my mouth but smiling at him when he looked my way.

'I go now. I will send car for you at 7pm. You come to my restaurant. I give you good food, make you better.'

I smiled again and thanked him for his kindness, stroking him on his arm. As he left, the girl reassured me they were going to wait ten minutes for him to go and then try to redress the foot.

'Good news,' I heard a distant cry. 'We have some Steri-Strips. They'll do the trick.'

Un- bandaging my foot, the other girl reassured me she had been first aid trained. Applying the strips to the split toe did seem to eventually stop the blood. Wrapping up my foot somewhat more professionally than the pretend doctor, I was pleased and sighed with relief. Maybe I will live to see another day.

Alex had been scrubbing the deck and scrubbing it again. All I could hear was him banging on about how it was like a massacre had taken place. It took him ages to get the boat clean and back to its original sparkling state.

At 7pm the vehicle arrived to take me to the restaurant. I had said to the hostess on the boat and Alex that I didn't really want to go. I was worried about it bleeding so I hobbled on the side of my foot, not wanting it to start pouring with blood again. I cringed as I walked and I kept looking down to see if there was more blood coming out over the dressing.

As we approached the road a van stood waiting for me. It was the son who'd brought the medication driving.

'You get in front,' he pointed at me.

'You get in back or walk up mountain,' he said as he poked his finger towards Alex.

'Is it ok for me to get in the back, please? I'd prefer not to walk.'

He signalled to Alex and nodded for him to go round the back.

I could hear Alex complaining as he opened the door.

'Oh, it's filthy in here.'

He clambered in but as I peered back through a metal guard I could see he was on all fours.

'What's wrong Alex? Just be grateful. Don't be so rude,' I laughed.

The young man turned the van around. As we climbed the mountain I could hear Alex's head bashing on the side of the van as we travelled screeching on hairpin bends.

'Poor Alex', I thought but couldn't help laughing.

The noises he was making as the van cork screwed its way up were hysterical. A near emergency stop on a bend had Alex reeling forward as he was still in the doggy position.

'Bugger, shit, arggghh, ouch.' More banging and bashing echoed through the van.

Pulling over, the young man got out from the van and opened the back up for Alex. As Alex emerged it was so funny. His knees, hands and forehead were black, covered in grease.

He walked round to my seat and the man said, 'we not at restaurant yet. I go further up. You lady come with me.'

He pointed to a horse trough on the side of the road to Alex. 'You wash here then walk more up.'

So off we went and I was being driven away by a complete stranger but I was still laughing. I could see Alex in the side mirror looking at me as he disappeared into the distance.

On arriving at the restaurant the doctor came running over to me.

'Lady, lady, you come. Sit here, I get you a seat for your foot and a wine.'

He helped me by cradling my elbow and gently shuffled me in a position at the end of a large table. He lifted my leg up and put it on a chair turned sideways. He patted me on the shoulder as he left and then returned with a large glass of chilled white wine.

I looked at my foot. Thankfully there was no blood seeping through the dressing.

Fifteen minutes later Alex arrived. Puffed and out of breath but smiling wildly as he approached me, we both burst out laughing. What a day! We had a lovely evening.

Now it was the end of the night and the young man had arrived, revving his motorbike up at the side of my table.

'Lady, you get on. I take you back to boat, no van now.'

I smiled and thought, 'Shit, this is not a good idea on those bends. I am so accident prone, we are bound to crash.'

Immediately the hostess from the lead boat came over as she could see I needed help.

'Oh no, do you not have the van? She can't go on that.'

'I have car, no van,' he grinned.

'Can you get the car please or we can get a taxi. That is a bit dangerous for her,' she said, shaking her head.

Five minutes later the car arrived and both Alex and I got back to the boat clean and safe.

We arrived back in England. Our holiday had been an adventure. When we left Greece, I had thanked the crew of the Sunsail flotilla for helping me. My foot had healed well and had not hindered the rest of the holiday,

After a couple of days at home I was on the phone sorting out the final arrangements for the crew to sail Serendipity. Since it was a new boat to us it would feel strange to sail her back. In fact, I was excited and apprehensive, as I believed the rest of the crew to be.

I arranged to go down to the boat on the Friday night before. Setting off on the early tide was the plan but we knew this proposal could change for many reasons, but mainly because of the weather.

It was time to clean Water Baby to get her ready to sell. I was alone polishing her wood. I mopped and waxed on deck, then rubbed her stainless steel until it gleamed. She twinkled in the sunshine.

I remained still, gently moving my eyes all over her, thinking of the times she had protected me in abysmal weather. I sighed, and sadness swept over me. I wondered who would buy this wonderful boat. Whoever did needed to take care of her as she was astoundingly special. Easing myself on to the back seat, I put my head into my hands.

I needed to sit and reflect on all I had ever done with Water Baby as soon she would be gone.

Can you love a boat? I mean actually love it? I'm feeling silly now but I think I have fallen in love with Water Baby and before long I will not be able to board her anymore. I will miss her so much.

Water Baby's appeal worked and within a week she was out of the water being surveyed by her potential owners. Both of us were determined to meet the prospective buyers. We'd jumped in the car and were heading towards Brighton. Hearing a faint ringing tone, I turned the car radio down and answered Alex's phone.

Funnily enough it was Matt the surveyor who assessed Serendipity for us. He was actually in the hull of Water Baby carrying out the survey for the possible buyers. There was urgency in his voice.

'We have a problem. I was testing the seacock in the engine compartment and unfortunately it's snapped off. The boat could sink!'

We've managed to put a bung in the hole to stop the water flow but we need a new seacock fitted and we need it now. There's a lot of water in the engine partition.'

'Oh, for crying out loud!' I shook my head.

'What's wrong?' Alex frowned.

'You won't believe what the bloody hell has happened now.'

I related Matt's words to Alex and he looked pretty pissed off.

'Fucking hell! Tell him we are on our way, I will mend it as soon as we get there and that's providing I can get the parts we need.'

We were in deep shock. Water Baby could have sunk with the new owners on board. Matt had confirmed they had been standing in the galley of Water Baby chatting to him when the seacock broke away.

Pulling up at the dockside, we stared over the wall down towards Water Baby. She was tethered to the concrete block. A middle aged lady looked up and smiled at me. Slowly I descended a slim steel ladder about 20 feet in length. With my hands slimed with smelly seaweed and mud, I triumphantly jumped onto the pontoon, wiping my hands down my jeans. The lady, who was brightly dressed, introduced herself as Macy and her partner, who was dressed in jeans and a checked shirt, was called Eddy. We shook their hands.

I could feel my face going red. I was quite embarrassed that Water Baby had suffered a serious leak.

Potentially, had they bought it, she could have failed at sea and without bungs it could have been fatal.

Eddy didn't seem deterred. He appeared enthusiastic considering we were trying to fix a big hole in the bottom of the boat. Funnily enough, last week I had watched a feature on broken seacocks.

To stop a boat sinking the two guys had performed trials, using carrots, potatoes and a thick grey putty from America. Ramming them all separately into the exposed hole to block the fountain of water to see which was the most effective. It evoked a sense of panic in me knowing that the seacock could have gone at any time, even when we were sailing back from the Solent in 38knots of wind and high seas. Water Baby had protected me.

Alex phoned the local chandlers and was lucky to get the right parts to replace the seacock. Water Baby was put into the slings to lift her out of the water and they smoothly placed her on a cradle so Alex could change the seacock without sinking her.

At the same time Matt continued to survey her underneath. I was sure after this fiasco that they were going to pull out of the sale. Surprisingly I was wrong. Macy and Eddie loved her. I knew they would take care of her as they both seemed smitten.

Down in the hull, Macy commented on the interior and how the boat had smelt of wood polish and air freshener. She told me that she had never been on a boat before that looked so clean and fresh. I plumped up the soft cushions. I felt very proud of Water Baby. I had cherished every inch of my pride and joy. Selling her for more than £1,000 more than we'd paid for her was a massive bonus.

Within the next two weeks Water Baby would be sailed across to France, leaving a gaping hole where she had been moored outside Ancasta. Now, all I retained were my memories.

Knowing Water Baby would be making the course to France the same day, we collected Serendipity. This occupied my thoughts as I was mindful that as we sailed one way, she would be heading seventy odd nautical miles in a southerly direction, whilst we would sail from West to East.

Josh, Robert, Alex and I gathered on Serendipity on the Friday night. This had been a challenge as all four of us had come from different areas such as London, Sussex, Kent and Surrey.

Firstly claiming our cabins for the night by throwing our bags on the beds, we settled around the table and shared a few drinks. Aware we had to get up extremely early we knew that having a skin full was not a sensible option.

Josh, Robert's son, repeatedly pulled Robert's leg.

'Yeah you're called Captain No Reef you are, or we could call you Captain Kamikaze. You're dangerous. It takes a hurricane for him to reef in.'

Josh threw back his head and laughed, waiting for the reprimand.

Robert just glared then popped, 'You should be Captain Curly'.

Josh grabbed his hair with both of his hands pulling it high into the air.

'We can call you Captain Belly'.

Josh shot a glance at Alex. I loved Alex's belly.

'It's cuddly,' I thought.

Alex smiled at me and I thought, 'Oh here we go. What will my name be?'

'Definitely Captain Panic,' he grinned.

He was right. I do panic and the amount of times I have cried at sea, the sea would never dry out!

I thought Robert was going to tick Josh off for criticising his sailing technique but luckily he just took it in good jest.

A couple of months ago I was talking to my son Max, chatting about how I hardly tell him off, but he astounded me when he said that most of the time I was placid but when I did have a go or quip him with a one liner, he declared that I would sometimes nuke him. I remembered feeling quite shocked as I always assumed I was quite light hearted even when I was illuminating his naughtiness. Clearly a nuke sounded a bit alarming but he couldn't give me an example, so nuke or no nuke, I came to the conclusion that it wasn't that bad after all.

'Does he tell you off much?' I questioned Josh.

'He might do but I take no notice of him.' Robert stuck his tongue out towards his son.

'Sounds like my sister's boys. They don't take much notice of her either.'

I explained that when my two lads had slept at her house one night with their two cousins it was bedlam. My son Joe arrived home the next day giggling away and proceeded to tell me that Kacie had been in and out of their bedroom asking them to be quiet. Undoubtedly they had completely ignored her as for about the fourth time she burst into their room at about 2am, flicking the light on in frenzy.

She raised her arm in the air like the fat controller from 'Thomas The Tank Engine' and repeatedly flexed her rigid arm up and down in clear definite chopping actions, screaming at the top of her voice, 'Respect me, respect me, respect me, respect me,' without taking a breath.

She then looked at them all as she gasped for air. All together they burst out laughing at her. She stood flummoxed for a few seconds and then she started to chuckle too. Apparently she couldn't move for laughing and eventually found her legs to go. The boys remember this incident well and often mention it.

I used to have such a giggle with my mum and to this day, as adults, we don't argue. I think I can remember her once getting angry and swiping me across the face but I can't recall what I had done. Because I enjoyed my mum's company I would often wind her up.

Marching up and down the supermarket one day, while we were gazing into the array of peas, a man stood feet away from us and I said in a very loud voice, 'Oh mum, why did you have sex with the postman?'

The man darted his face towards mum, giving her a dirty look.

'You little devil,' she said, pushing her elbow into my ribs as I reached down to grab a bag of peas. As she shoved me, my false finger nail fell off and got stuck on top of one of the frozen bags. I pointed at it, hooting with laughter.

'Pick it up,' she gestured.

'No I think I'll leave it there. It will be funny when someone has to scrutinise it to work out what it is. A bag of frozen peas and a free finger nail.'

I screwed up my nose and giggled.

On a different occasion, both mum and I were squashed into a tube train. I was about fourteen years old. We were chatting across the aisle when someone had clearly farted. Talk about the 'English stiff upper lip'. Everyone was pretending that it had not happened, continuing to read their newspaper with blank expressions on their faces.

I offered my opinion, in a somewhat expressive tirade.

'Oh my word! Who has farted? Why are you all pretending that no one's dropped one? The smell is atrocious. Come on, own up. Who's done it? Say 'Pardon me'.'

My mother told me to be quiet but I just stood up and addressed the carriage.

'OK, so who did that then?' It was absurdly funny. So many people put their heads down and pretended I wasn't there. Eventually I did sit down, but not before I had made it quite clear that the person who'd farted was disgusting and I had announced that I was speaking for the whole of the stunk out compartment. I would never do that today. I'm a lot quieter now.

Once I had calmed down I stared around the train carriage and spotted a man carrying about a hundredweight of toilet rolls. Funnily enough a few days before my mum had been shopping and she'd purchased twenty four toilet rolls and while she was unloading her boot and taking the shopping into the house, some arse had stolen them.

Her car had been parked on the drive and she'd only been in the house a minute. As she came out she could see a man running away, with mum's toilet rolls clamped under his arms. I tried to convince her that the chap on the train was her toilet roll thief. All I can say is someone at home must have had a problem. No one needs that many loo rolls.

Back on the boat I regrettably informed the crew, 'No more booze tonight lads. Let's get an early night. A 4am start won't be much fun.'

Waking up to Alex farting intermittently, I knew it was definitely the morning.

'You could never find anyone else to put up with that performance,' I muttered a little discontented.

'Good morning. Just performing my love chorus for you,'

Cheerily he waded into the galley for breakfast.

179

Every day when I wake up, my first thought is for a nice cup of tea. I don't function without the caffeine. I have to feel that circulating in my blood before I can get going.

Outside it was pitch black. I stood on deck and gazed around me. It looked scary. I peered in the direction of the passage out but I could not see any markers to show the channel.

'Blimey it's dark out there. You can't see anything.'

Everyone else scrambled on deck and agreed it did appear somewhat daunting.

Casting off we took it slowly as we were heading out towards the sea.

Motoring down the murky strait and out into the Southampton water, we were all fairly quiet. At this point we were not sailing. We navigated towards the Calshot cardinal marker and then turned towards Portsmouth.

Everything on the boat seemed strange. Even the GPS was difficult to use. It was very different to Water Baby's navigation equipment. Alex was struggling to make the damn thing work, despite trying to familiarise himself with it before we departed.

We were trying to follow the North Channel but we were completely unfamiliar with the depth gauge. The plotter kept turning off for some reason. It was scary for us all and frantic chatter filled the air as we tried to decipher where we actually were. In an instant, the depth alarm shrilled out.

'Flipping heck, we're out of the channel and could run aground.'

Each of us was shouting out suggestions to rectify the problem and mine was to turn right around and trace our track back. At least we knew, as we'd motored along that stretch already, that the depth had been fine. If we went port or starboard then potentially we could be in serious trouble.

I was pleased when the men actually listened to me and we swung her around and traced ourselves back as best as we could. Now and again the depth alarm sounded but straightening her up did the trick and we got back to the Calshot Cardinal.

Discussing the only option we had left, Serendipity was directed gingerly towards the main channel. Our fears were the big liners and carriers dominating the waters of the main channel. In pitch black conditions, we had our navigation lights on but night sailing still felt slightly alarming in an unfamiliar boat.

I didn't want a repeat of when the Pride of Bilbao came steaming towards us, lighting us up like a Christmas tree.

Once in the main channel we gained our bearings and the GPS started to behave itself. In an hour or so it would start to become light. I relished the thought. Ahead of us was about a ten hour sail to get Serendipity back to our home port.

'I'll make a cup of tea before we get the sails out and the boat starts to heel.'

Thumping towards the gas locker, I lifted up the heavy lid. After turning on the gas I made my way down to the galley. Opening the cupboards and trying to remember where everything was stored became confusing. Water Baby's storage was much bigger as we'd had one less cabin and a far bigger galley kitchen.

Sorting through each one I found where the cups had been stored. I lit the gas burner and bent down to get the kettle when I heard a fizzle and a terrible smell.

'Ohhhh!' I squealed, bashing the top of my head. I ran the tap and threw water over my head. I was panicking. I ran to the mirror.

'Oh fuck it. I've singed the top of my hair. I am lucky I have not completely set it on fire,' I bellowed up on deck.

'Let's look'.

They all hustled to get a gloat.

Why do men have such sick sense of humour? What ensued was a torrent of them haranguing me. There were jokes about Medusa and how I now looked so much better with the front of my hair burnt off.

Oh boy that made me so irritable! Rather than placing their teas in their hands, I felt like throwing it in their faces and getting my own back but as I am such a kind, loving, caring and sharing person I decided to let their quips go in one ear and out the other.

My back was itching as I emerged from down below and found a nice part of the companionway to sidle up to backwards and use as a scratching post. I was in heaven, moving up and down, from side to side, just like Baloo the bear from the Jungle book.

'She's like a grizzly bear. She looks scary enough with that new hairdo,' one of them piped up.

Then I decided my backside was itching too so I bent forward and continued to rub my bum on the wood, enjoying every minute.

'Oh what the hell are you doing?'

Alex shook his head.

I proceeded to explain that when you have several pairs of trousers on and all your sailing gear, getting to scratch your bum isn't easy and I was in heaven

'This is our new boat. Stop that,' Alex begged.

I laughed loudly and the lads thought it was funny too as I continued to rub my bum up and down the wood.

Water Baby had in-mast reefing and Serendipity sported slab reefing, so to hoist the sail we had to release the reefs manually by unclamping the jam cleats and feeding them through slowly, as we heaved the sail up. One brilliant feature was an electric winch, something Water Baby didn't have. So, after pulling the sail through the jackstays, employing the electric winch was easy. Pulling out the genoa, we were now on our way. It was peaceful but our start had been none too easy.

The horizon loomed as it became lighter. Fluffy grey clouds scattered the sky as the day was breaking and a slight reddish tinge flanked the sky. It was cold though and we gathered together for a chat

Alex was helming. Babble gratified us, as we had many more hours ahead.

'Do you think you will get another dog?' Josh asked.

'No, not now we have the new boat. As much as I loved Hooch, towards the end it became so difficult managing to sail and making sure we cared for him properly.'

Hooch had been so special and just before the end of his life I became so worried. I could tell he was in pain when he lay down, and taking him to the vets encountered lead pulling, barking, salivating and general discontent. I tried to convey my fears that I was sure there was more to Hooch's illness than arthritis.

I was so insistent when I took Hooch back to the vet that the vet performed an x-ray on him. The vet prodded his tummy hard, lifting him up on his belly just below his rib cage. Within seconds of him wrenching on his gut there were big farting noises. I was quite shocked.

'Is that him?' I asked very concerned.

'Well it's not me, is it?'

The vet looked surprised and glanced at me under his dark rimmed glasses.

'Sorry,' I said, looking sheepish.

On being told he needed an operation I knew it was serious but as I cuddled Hooch in my arms, I told him I loved him. I didn't realise it would be the last time I would hold his big soft furry body in my arms.

'Bye Hoochie. See you soon sweetie pie. I love you.'

I waved and smiled at him but I could see he was frightened. A few hours later my phone rang.

'I am sorry, Hooch is on the operating table now but he is riddled with cancer through his liver and lungs. It's best we let him go.'

Numb, I agreed, put the phone down and burst into tears. My Hoochie Poochie! I will never cuddle him again. I won't see him wagging his tail and rolling his soft ears in my hands.

I phoned Alex sobbing my eyes out and he came straight home to be with me. Alex's eyes were reddened too. We cuddled each other in our grief. Josh could see just talking about Hooch had stirred many emotions and I wiped a tear away from my eye.

Changing the subject, Josh spoke softly.

'Ok, so the new boat takes over. Where do you guys see yourselves going in her?'

'Maybe this summer we'll get to Jersey and Guernsey, weather permitting of course, and if I feel confident enough to go.'

A few raised eyebrows endorsed my lengthy struggles.

Pouring out the wine, I giggled as I lifted the third glass to my lips. The men were slurping bottles of lager. A random big wave hit the side of the boat and as it did I fell backwards with my legs up in the air. I lifted my arm high into the air trying to save the contents of my wine glass. I couldn't establish myself in an upright position and as I rolled around the back of the boat, laughter got the better of me and I was doing my usual pig snorting.

'Be careful. You'll go over if you're not careful,' Alex scolded me.

Still lying on my back I told him I was fine. Sometimes I just love drinking wine. It throws away any fear and I occasionally feel invincible. I asked Robert to take my wine glass and I started to do tummy exercises, lifting my legs high into the air.

'Will you get up?'

Alex grabbed my coat by the collar and dragged me into a sitting position. Finally I showed him I was stable and behaved myself by asking for my wine glass back. After all, I wasn't going to spill that was I?

After sailing past Portsmouth we sailed out to the Forts, avoiding the submarine barrier. I hoped to see dolphins again at Selsey Bill but they didn't show. Sailing on from there we passed Bognor and on to Shoreham. Most of the journey encompassed calm conditions, but the odd blow here and there made no significance to our progress.

Over the radio we could hear a Mayday call. It appeared that someone had run aground at Bramble Bank near the Solent.

'Oh dear someone has their bottom stuck!' I screamed.

Seriously though, the Coastguards do the most fantastic job. The RNLI are unsung heroes. So many lives are saved every year and all by volunteers. I always give towards the cause if I have any spare money when I see them collecting.

Once we heard on the radio that a car had gone over the cliff but the volunteers had to try to establish if anyone was in the vehicle. Hours and hours later it was reported that the car had been pushed over. Luckily no one was inside. It really angered me that someone would waste people's time like that.

Sailors are extraordinarily lucky to have such brave and dedicated people who give their time for nothing. My respect goes out to all the emergency services paid or volunteers.

Josh was practicing tying knots, something I still unrelentingly found problematic. Once Max had kindly sat with me for hours teaching me a bowline knot, only for him to tell me the next day what he had taught me was a load of rubbish. It wasn't a bowline. I was not amused. I'd been boasting and demonstrating to my colleagues at work how I could tie one. What an idiot I believed myself to be. Thankfully no one knew it was a sham and I left my bit of string at home the next day, deciding I need not embarrass myself yet again.

Our passage had been a real mixture of fun, boredom and determination. Reaching Brighton, tiredness raged through us all and driving home didn't seem like a good idea so we stayed on the boat. As Serendipity was 4 feet longer than Water Baby we had to pay for a lengthier berth.

Several of the boats around us looked a little tired compared to Serendipity which was spanking new. She attracted a lot of attention. A few fellow sailors came over and entered into a chat about how gorgeous she was. I felt really proud to own her. She was rather special and I hoped the future would be a positive one.

Safely tied up and the electric plugged in to keep the dehumidifier going, we left Serendipity and headed home. Time for us to contemplate our next sailing trip, when and where would we go?

AGEING, OUR FIGHT FOR LIFE

Alex was starting a new job today. He wore his smart black suit. He went to get his new shoelaces that he'd bought for his clean shoes.

I could see him threading the laces through the shoes but couldn't believe my eyes when he was threading brown shoe laces into black shoes.

'Can you not see there's a problem?' I questioned him.

He scrutinised what he was doing and replied 'No'.'

'Alex, they are brown shoe laces, you silly devil.'

I pulled at the shoe he had in his hand.

'They're not are they?'

'Yes they are. When did you buy them?'

What with shouting at a brown dog and now brown shoe laces I was beginning to wonder if he was losing it. Luckily we found some black ones and threaded them in.

Getting old is horrible. Driving Alex to the train station I kissed him goodbye and went home to get breakfast. As I opened the front door I could hear the phone ringing. It was Gina one of my oldest friends.

'Alana, I need to talk to you. Have you got time?' I could hear urgency in her voice.

'Yes of course I've got time, what's wrong?'

'I'm getting old. I've just had a terrible experience. I was showering and the hot water flowed across my body and I bubbled myself up with a coconut body scrub. Singing out loud, I stepped onto the bathroom mat and was drying myself off with a fluffy towel when I glanced down towards my legs. Then I saw it!' she bellowed. She then continued, 'I stared down in disbelief looking at my muff. I was petrified. Had I just seen a grey pubic hair? I ruffled myself with the towel again, glaring harder. I was in shock, and it

187

definitely was a grey pubic hair. I didn't even know that you went grey down there.' She was flustered.

I started laughing, then she continued, 'I quickly wrapped myself tight with a towel and ran into the lounge. I grabbed the phone and dialled my mum's number. "You alright Gina?" my mum asked me. "No mum, I am so upset. Can I ask you a question?" I was sure she could sense the panic in my voice. "Oh mum, do you go grey down there?" I asked her. "Do what, what did you just say?" she said.' Gina was barely taking a breath.

She carried on. 'So I asked her again "Mum does it go grey down there? Does your muff go grey?" Suddenly my mum started really laughing Alana. She replied, "You silly date. Of course it does." I was so upset and kept repeating that I never ever thought about that happening and that I was shocked.' I grimaced at the mental picture.

She described the aftermath, 'Coming off the phone I ran back into the bathroom and looked at my reflection, I boomed at the mirror, "Knock a woman when she's down." I studied my face. I loathe getting old. I am having a sad day Alana. My body's changing and there is nothing I can do about it. Have your bits started to sag, go grey and travel south?'

'Oh dear Gina, you are having a bad day aren't you sweetheart? And the answer is, no not yet and to be honest I am as shocked about that as you are. I didn't know you go grey down there either. Well that's something for me to look forward to. I didn't want to know that,' I laughed. 'Want to have a cuppa to calm you down?' An hour later she popped over for a coffee and I consoled her.

What is it about getting old that makes you do ridiculous things and make such awful mistakes? I was driving the car with four of my friends. We were off to do a scuba dive. I peered towards the Sussex Downs (an area of hilly countryside) and we could see a plane flying very low.

I commented on how I thought it looked like it could possibly be a Cessna out of control and maybe was about to crash. All of us gazed in its direction and then we saw it disappear behind a hill and then there was a lot of smoke.

I was convinced the plane had crashed and the smoke was the aftermath. All the girls agreed and we decided that we needed to call the police. As I was at the wheel I suggested Zoe make the call. She explained to them what had happened. They took her details and gave her a good grilling about what we had witnessed and they thanked her and said they would investigate. She did feel a bit concerned when she came off the phone that the police officer had been a little too questioning. His manner had made her feel uncomfortable. He said he would be back in touch with her.

Four women thinking they had just watched a plane go down resulted in a wave of anxious ranting. We blabbered about each other's interpretation of events. About two hours after our dive, we were returning home when Zoe's phone rang. It was the police. They wanted to inform us that they had investigated the information we had given them and the plane had landed safely. With regard to the smoke, someone in the vicinity had lit a big bonfire.

Zoe's eyes grew as they were talking to her.

'Oh how silly,' she screamed as she came off the phone, 'what a load of plonker's we are.'

Zoe explained that apparently there was a small landing strip in the Downs and that was where the plane had landed and a farmer had stoked up an outside fire. We laughed at our assessment of events and how hysterically wrong we had all been.

Another funny time was when we girls had flown to Nice and stayed in a wonderful hotel along the sea front. Venturing out during the day we had caught the bus to Monaco. On the way back we stopped for a meal. A handsome waiter smiled at me and called me charming.

'If only he knew how mad I am at times', I thought.

We were waiting at a bus stop to get back to the hotel. Chirpy and bright we waited patiently for the bus. We waited and waited. About an hour and a half later we'd started to moan about how long the bus was taking and our legs were starting to hurt. Finally there was a big cheer from us all as the bus arrived.

Jumping on, we marched to the back of the bus and sat down on the dirty seats. None of us knew where we were and I had suggested we get off when we saw the sea front and then we could walk along.

After about twenty minutes on the bus Zoe shouted, 'That's the back of our hotel. Quick let's get off.'

'Are you sure?' I quizzed her.

It didn't seem as if the sea was anywhere to be seen.

'Yes get off, get off.' She said, shuffling us all onto the pavement. We scanned the area.

'I don't think we are anywhere near the sea Zoe.'

I shook my head. Moaning again, we asked a passer-by. The sea was miles away. We had no choice but to keep walking. The bus had been the last of the evening.

On every corner of the street were lady boys, touting for business. It felt a little unnerving. I must admit some of them looked stunning. They had better figures than us. Their skirts were really short and they were wearing long false eyelashes. They flashed us a smile as we walked by.

We women found it fascinating. It was a fixation which kept us going on the long hike back to the hotel. As we strolled down each road it was like a surprise on the next corner. To this day we all pull Zoe's leg about her get off the bus scenario.

Back at the hotel we took some fantastic pictures all pretending to be struck by lightning on the balcony. It was comical. To finish off we did a group photo of all being struck by lightning, lying draped over the sofa with our legs and arms flailing out and piled on top of each other. I love being with my friends and they are all different in their own way.

We put some music on. I loved to see Stephanie dancing; she gets so carried away and loses herself in the music. Her face contorts in a nice way as she moves to the rhythm. Her lips puckering as she savours the feeling of moving to the beat.

The next day we went into a shop to buy some mints and Megan was standing behind a man ordering some cigarettes. He asked in French for some Gitane cigarettes and Megan stepped outside convinced he had been asking for a shit and cigarettes. She'd been very observant. We cackled.

I recall another time when we girls were at the casino at Brighton marina. I was feeling in a particularly cheesed off mood that evening and we had gone into the toilet in the casino. A woman was in the toilet applying her lipstick.

'Do you know what time it is?' she asked me.

I looked and shouted, 'It's sex time.'

She started to really laugh. Kacie was with me and we both sniggered but the woman seemed to think it was extra side splitting and started jolting her head backwards and forwards with massive chortles and suddenly her wig fell off.

I lost it completely and so did Kacie. I even picked the wig up off the floor and handed it back to her. She was sweet really and as she tried to position her wig back on her head, we stayed with her until she'd sorted it out.

Back home Alex and I enthusiastically planned the weekend ahead. We would get to Brighton early and sail to Eastbourne. Vamoosing out on the tide in a force four and on a south westerly wind we should be flying along on a run, arriving early afternoon and off for a nice meal in the evening.

Radio check completed, we cast off. Sailing from Brighton to Eastbourne is a relatively simple passage. I felt a chilled air and the sea looked grey. Squinting towards France I could see a thick blanket of cloud fringe the skyline. Wrapped up in our sailing kit, I helmed Serendipity while Alex was up at the bow trying to sort out a rigging problem. I gripped the wheel and she responded so much more easily than Water Baby. Only small movements would send her in a different direction. I knew reversing her was harder and I could see hours of practice ahead. Checking the GPS I was doing really well and on course, I felt I was handling her perfectly.

Ahead, a few flying fish were leaping out of the water, as if someone had catapulted them into the air. Just off Newhaven and Seaford fishing trawlers were engulfed by hundreds of swooping seagulls catching the fish guts as the fisherman threw them out and discarded them.

Bobbing about on a force 4 wind and three foot waves, it was an easy sail until we made our approach towards Beachy Head.

Within ten minutes the wind direction and speed started to change. From a south westerly it had swung round, now blowing a southerly, and had increased to a force six, verging on a seven. Huge waves that resembled a wall pounded us. I was really frightened, even more than being in the strong winds and nearly running out of fuel coming back from the Solent.

I had to crane my neck to see the top of the waves. They remained persistent and dangerous at least 12 to 15 feet high. As the weather had changed so quickly, we had not even reefed in and were still on full sails. It was vitally important that we did not let the waves hit us directly on the side or it would be a disaster. Another added complication was that we had to sail so that the rollers hit us at the back but to one side. If we had turned completely so the waves could hit us directly on the stern we would have been sailing towards the rocks just off the Beachy Head lighthouse.

I was petrified. I was at the helm as Alex battled with the sails trying to get them in. They were blowing everywhere. As we had been on a run Alex had tied a preventer on to the mainsail. The rigging was tangling and Alex had to clip on a lifeline as he needed to head down to the bow to untangle something which had hooked up. I never knew I could cope in such awful circumstances. I wrestled with my emotional state. My heart was thumping in my chest. I was conscious that if I cocked this up we could die at sea and this was reality and not a dream.

I kept glancing behind me as yet more barrages of water towered high, throwing themselves at us. I was soaked, my hair stuck to my head and it seemed as if we were fighting for our lives. It was impossible to sail so that the waves hit precisely to the stern.

I was watching the GPS closely and I was aware that we were close to the rocks but if we turned the other way we could suffer a knockdown.

Alex persisted up on the bow. I frantically shouted to him to hold on and be careful. If he went overboard then there was no way he could survive.

Our only hopes were either for the waves and winds to die down or to manage to get into the shelter of Eastbourne Bay. Ultimately, Alex finally unhooked the rope and in due course we managed to furl in the genoa and then drop the final part of the mainsail a tiny bit at a time, lastly pulling the reefs in tight.

Then, after half an hour in the extremes, our battle was finally over, moving into the calmer waters of Eastbourne Bay; the nightmare had ended.

I never ever want to experience that again in my life. It was like something from a movie - just make believe. Walls of water were coming at us. I can't describe it any other way. They towered so high that I found it hard to believe it was real, even though I had lived through it.

The sea started to calm down and I burst into tears as we limped into Eastbourne marina. The serious nature of what we had just encountered hit me hard. My emotions wobbled from being proud that I had coped, to crying because we could have died.

It's bizarre, when environments alter and you are at sea, there are no choices. You just have to deal with it. As we entered the lock I was already fretting about our return trip the next day. The visitors' pontoons are on the left as you enter Eastbourne Marina and luckily we moored next to a boat with two dogs on board.

I love fussing dogs and I think I could live entirely with dogs and no humans and still be happy. I cuddled two big Labradors which brought me instant comfort.

When we were tied up safely I headed towards the shower block and thought longingly about a large glass of wine. My balance was weird. I was wobbling about on my feet and I felt as if I was still at sea.

Returning from the showers, my mood changed and I felt quite triumphant at how I had managed to survive in such dreadful circumstances. Alex was stood at one of the wheels and I leapt onto the boat, ran over and grabbed the back of his shorts pulling them and his pants right down round his ankles. He bent straight down to pull them up and hit his head on the wheel.

Squealing with laughter, I became hyper as Alex cautioned me. Snatching some drinks from the fridge I brought them up on deck. Sipping the wine diminished my stress levels and I nestled into a cushion.

Alex sat opposite me and appeared to be engrossed staring at something behind me.

'Are you perving?' I demanded.

He started to chortle.

'You have to be joking. I am actually watching a big bald fat man who is running and looks as if he has shit himself.'

I crooked my neck to appreciate the vision and yes, it did seem that he might have crapped himself. Just the two of us on deck made a change so Alex came over and cuddled up to me. General chit chat followed.

I enlightened Alex with the fact that I was fretful that he had gotten into the habit of not bending down to take his socks off at night. Every bedtime he would stand at the bottom of the bed and drag his socks off by running his foot hard into the floor using the carpet to slip off his socks.

'Listen; if you keep on executing your sock ritual, eventually you won't be able to bend down to take your socks off. You'll be too stiff in the body. In the long run you will seize up and won't be able to perform sexual acts.'

Seeing Alex defending his sock procedure was very funny. Trying to reassure me that his sexual performance would not be compromised because of his socks was hilarious.

Two fishermen plodded along the pontoon with their catch.

'What did you get today?' I enquired.

Stopping, they showed me their bucket. It was full of large plaice.

'Wow, what a catch. Bet you had a lovely time. Did you get caught in those big waves?'

'No we don't go out too far. We were Just off the beach about half a mile.'

I enjoyed chatting to them and one described two octopi he'd seen. One was dancing whilst waiting in the water while they released the other one from their net. It sounded so sweet. They are very graceful in the sea with their tentacles flowing like the streams of a silk dress.

Sitting in the cosy restaurant, I clamped my hands between my knees and I asked Alex, 'Do you want a Chinese beer?'

'Err no,' he griped.

'Oh why's that then?'

'Because we're in an Indian restaurant.'

Smirking, he lifted the menu to his face, and then peered over the top of it straight at me. I playfully bashed the menu.

'Let's have some wine,' I said, choosing a nice chilled Sauvignon Blanc which we subsequently savoured between us.

Holding hands across the table, we jawed about our sail that day. Alex seemed calm but I am almost certain that the size of the waves would have put the wind up him in more ways than one.

MATT DAMON, IS THAT YOU?

Today had been extremely scary.

Deep down, I knew I could not give up. I had an inbuilt determination that whatever I do, I'd never give up. So many times in my life I had faced challenges and they had made me stronger.

Strolling back to the boat that evening was peaceful. The forecast for the next day was favourable. Putting my arms around Alex, I cuddled him tightly and soon he was snoring. As I lay in bed my mind wandered.

I thought back to a couple of years ago when I had become fed up with counselling. I had spent five years at the rehab, a year as a domestic violence outreach worker, a year as a Probation Service Officer working on the Drug Treatment and Testing Orders and two years as a parent support/outreach advisor. I was burnt out.

As a little girl I had watched Bette Davis and Marilyn Monroe in the black and white films that I loved so much. I'd always wanted to be an actress but I'd put having children and marriage before my dreams. Plus my parents could never have afforded to send me to drama school.

A light flicked on. Do something for you, I encouraged myself.

I joined some agencies to work as a supporting artist on TV, films and commercials. One was called Casting Network run by Lesley Gogarty. In my opinion this was an excellent agency. Luckily I'd also replied to the 'This Morning' programme as they'd said on TV that they could do with ladies of varying ages to volunteer for a weekly running feature on beauty products and services.

I was picked as one of them. Live on TV, I was lying on a treatment couch covered in a foul smelling fishy body mask. I hated it. Phillip Schofield came over and asked me what I thought.

'It smells similar to a gone off prawn. It's disgusting. Never in a million years would I do this to myself.'

I screwed my nose up. When I had finished at the studios they had a car waiting to take me back home to Sussex.

I people watched from the window as we drove through the streets of London. My phone rang.

'Hello, is that Alana?' I didn't recognise the number or voice.

'It's the Casting Network. We were wondering if you could attend an audition tomorrow in London. It's for a part in a film as a barmaid. The director has seen your picture and wants to meet you. It's very exciting you know. The director is Robert de Niro.'

I went quiet. Was this one of my friends pissing about?

Tentatively I trod carefully.

'What hotel do I go to and what time is it please?'

Did Robert de Niro really want to see me? I questioned myself.

I seriously thought that this was a wind up but took all the details down in full and when I checked the agency number I thought, 'Shit it really is a real audition'.

I'd watched Robert De Niro as a little girl. My father and brothers had been great fans of his films when I was in my teens. He always came across on screen as a real hard man. The films had an abundance of killing and shooting in them.

I rang all my friends and family. I was so excited. I had visions of becoming the new Bette Davis or Marilyn Munroe.

Later on in the afternoon I had another phone call. The audition had been moved to the pub where they would be filming on location.

On arriving I found that it was a seedy little pub. Not the sort of place I would go. I was booked in by a young lady. I took my place in line, butterflies attacking my tummy. My hair was blonde and curly. I wore red lipstick and a fairly low top with red ruffles.

Commotion commenced and a lot of bustling at the entrance of the pub revealed Robert De Niro walking along towards a line of us. Each and every one of us endured him staring at us from top to bottom. I didn't know if I should smile or stay serious but as his eyes wandered up and over me, I felt slightly awkward and looked away so as not to meet his gaze. He was so much smaller than I had imagined. As he plays quite violent characters on screen I assumed that he was tall and strong but in fact he was quite short and wore a baseball hat.

Within minutes we were hustled out of the pub and told we would be contacted. Daydreaming on the train home, my phone rang. It was the agency.

Although I had not been picked to play the barmaid, I had been selected to be a supporting artiste on the film, 'The Good Shepherd' which Robert de Niro was definitely directing. Again I rang all my mates and family. It was the most exciting thing that had ever happened to me.

We were filming at the disused tube station in Aldwych and the story was set in World War Two. I had been dressed in a 1940s costume and my hair was made into side rolls which were tucked into a blue patterned head scarf.

The scene was supposed to be us running down a spiral staircase as an air raid was taking place above ground. It felt eerily real. We were told not to look at the cameras on the way down but it was not easy. Seeing where your footing needed to be placed took a bit of practice and as I ran down the stairs, suddenly a camera would appear.

I stood next to one of the main actors, who had appeared in a well-known children's film. I watched him. He didn't come across very well as he was a little grumpy.

There were a few children in the scene but when they asked him if he'd played a particular character he just kept a straight face said it wasn't him. I didn't know the other man who was stood next to him but he was chatting to him and he seemed receptive to his conversation.

I felt sorry for the kids. They were only little and their excitement and interest in him stood out as they spoke to each other. In my opinion he didn't need to be so short with such little children. It wasn't very nice.

After standing on the steps for a couple of hours doing take after take after take, the man who had been chatting to the unpleasant actor was now stood right next to me.

'How are you today?' he enquired.

'I'm OK thanks. How about you, how are you?'

'Oh I am not too bad. I did wake up with a cold but I am feeling a little better now,' he smiled.

'I am pleased about that. It's awful when you have to work and you're feeling low,' I empathised.

Suddenly this woman butted in and directed a question at me.

'Don't you think you're being a bit personal?' she grunted.

'I was only asking how he was in reply to his question. I'm just chatting. That's what people do,' I frowned at her and ignored her comment even though I did feel rather embarrassed. Cheeky cow! I shuffled nearer the young man.

'I travelled from Sussex today. My sons will miss me not being there at home.'

I smiled. I liked his face. It bore a soft expression when he replied.

'Yes I have a step daughter. Well her mum and I are not married yet but I love her like my own and I really miss her too.'

'Wow, that's so sweet. I bet she misses you too.'

'Yes I love her mum so much. She means everything to me.'

I warmed to this guy. He was fantastic - open, kind and caring. I'd been lucky to share his company.

Again this woman tugged on my arm, pulling me to one side.

'You are being too forward. Do you realise who that is?' she whispered.

'No, I have no idea who he is. We are just passing time.'

Looking sternly at me she told me that his name was Matt Damon, a very famous American actor and she said that under the agency agreement I should not be approaching him.

I reminded her that he spoke to me first. I tried to move away from her. Quite frankly I didn't care. To me he was a human being doing a job like me and we were having a natter which he had instigated.

The cameras were rolling again and after about eight hours of standing next to Matt we changed scenes. He was one of the most genuine men I have ever met. What a wonderful man to be so unspoilt and loving.

When I got home and told Joe, Max and Alex who I'd been talking to most of the day they couldn't believe it as they'd seen most of his action packed movies whereas I hadn't seen any of them.

I've watched them now and maybe if I'd known it was him I wouldn't have spoken to him. But hey, I did out of courtesy and he was a real gem of a man. He may be an actor but he is just another human being, like me.

I filmed for thirty six hours on 'The Good Shepherd' and I spent many hours in the freezing night sky running from the end of the road to the other, depicting the race for shelter during air raids in the war.

Anticipating the release of the film was purgatory. I waited for over a year for it to come out and as I sat in the cinema, my stomach churned with the expectation of me being on the screen.

Here comes the scene. There was Matt Damon running down the stairs and there was a wisp of my hair at the side of him. It was seconds and just a tuft of blonde, nothing else. Not me, not an arm or a leg. I was heartbroken. I sunk into my chair forlorn. All the months I had waited. And all there was to show was just a little blonde wisp.

Later on in the film I did see myself but I was silhouetted against the night sky running arm in arm with another supporting artiste. So that was it. My claim to fame was torn down in seconds but my fond memories of Matt will never die. The girlfriend he had is now his wife. She's a lucky lady.

I'd love to take part in a comedy. What a hoot that would be. So I have just written to Ricky Gervais' agent but their reply was a rebuff. They wouldn't forward my details to him.

Not only do I have a great CV for my crisis work I also have a fab CV now for TV, film and commercials. I have taken part in lots of adverts such as Coca Cola, Phones 4 U, Ford Mondeo, EDS Electrical and an O2 corporate video. The films I have been selected for and have appeared on are: 'Houdini', 'Miss Pettigrew for a day', 'Angus, Thongs and perfect Snogging', 'Young Victoria', 'Shoot on Sight' and 'Capturing Mary'.

I couldn't believe one director's behaviour. He was very expressive with his language and swearing. He appeared bad tempered. I think that his directing has gone to his head.

On these shoots you are often requested to wear your own clothes. Some poor man had a jumper on that he didn't like. He made him remove it and humiliated him by shouting out and swearing that it was disgusting and threw it on the floor behind a chair.

'Action!' he bellowed.

I started to walk on cue down the corridor but my shoes clip clopped on the floor.

'Whose making that noise on my set?' he boomed and shouted to the Assistant Director to pull me out and replace me.

Now I understand that you need to be focused when directing but I think he could do with some etiquette lessons. If he'd have sworn at me like he did the man with the terrible jumper, I'd have shouted back at him to stuff his film firmly right up his rear end. No way would he scream at me like that and get away with it, regardless of how important he thinks he is.

I once wrote to the Queen and complained to her about a chef who had been given an OBE. I ranted about how his swearing and techniques in getting people to tow-the-line were questionable. The Queen wrote back explaining that it was not her was responsibility to put people forward for an OBE and it had not been her doing.

Another call I received, from a different agency. 'Good morning Alana. We have a super job for you working in Portsmouth shopping centre. It's an MI5 training video. Do you think you can make it?'

'What are the dates?' I asked.

I set off for a two hour journey and wondered what the day would hold.

'This video is to help people escape under an attack in a shopping centre. We need you to listen very carefully.

We are setting off lots of pyrotechnics and people can get hurt. I need volunteers to throw themselves onto the floor when the bombs go off?'

A large crowd of supporting artistes had gathered as instructed but not one volunteered. I examined the men in the group, thinking one would pipe up but they just stood silent.

I stepped forward.

'OK, I'll do it.'

'Look, you men should be ashamed,' he admonished them.

'This lone young lady fearlessly comes forward. Surely one of you can help?'

A bearded chap stepped forward. Perched on a bench in the precinct as the bomb went off, I was told I had to launch myself into the sky and sprawl over the floor, covering my head with my hands coughing and spluttering.

'Boom!' The noise rang in my ears as I leaped into the air holding my shopping bags and then collapsing on the floor, sprawling like a star fish. Then I lay still.

Debris from the pyrotechnics filled the air and bits of black sponge were falling down round me, fake smoke pouring over me. I couldn't help but cough with all the crap floating about. My hands were blackened. I was covered in some sort of black soot. Over and over we filmed and one important message I gained from this filming is that if you are ever in a bomb attack do not run. If you can, crouch down where you are into a ball and cover your head with your hands.

I was informed during the making of the video that often bomb routes are planned so that when one goes off, your immediate reaction is to run, but normally you would run into the next explosion, so stay still.

It seems odd that an ordinary housewife could get involved in the making of such a video but it was an experience I will never forget.

I have been on Eastenders eating an ice cream in Brighton and I loved going on Noel's House party and getting gunged. Leslie Grantham, who played Dirty Den in Eastenders years ago, was standing in the Green Room, enjoying the BBC hospitality; I was engaged in a conversation with him.

I studied his clothes. He wore a dark green three piece suit, a light green shirt, dark green shoes and a green tie.

'You look like a cucumber,' I smiled at him cheekily.

Flushed red cheeks flashed back.

'Sorry. It's just you appear very green today, wouldn't you agree.'

He found it amusing being called a cucumber. We had a good laugh. Noel covered us completely in cold wet gunge. I even sung 'Moon River' with Noel Edmonds but sadly he said I sounded like a strangled cat, so my Lady Gaga days are over.

I'd appeared fourteen times as an unpaid volunteer on the This Morning programme, with Phillip Schofield, Fern Brittan, Eamon Holmes and his wife Ruth.

I loved going to the studio and taking part.

'Oh we are doing a slot on teeth whitening. Can you come down immediately? We need some before shots?'

'Yes OK. Be there was soon as I can.'

A two hour train journey later and I arrived at the studio. I was hustled in and plonked in front of a camera.

'Smile,' she said.

'OK, you can go now.'

Each few weeks they would do a live piece with four women all reflecting different age groups and we'd try out different beauty products. Various shows included evaluations of nail varnish, hair remover, facial creams and many more items. Often the products would be sent to our homes for the trial period before appearing. I thoroughly enjoyed my time there and did write afterwards asking if they had any permanent jobs but sadly they had enough presenters. It was a good creative programme which had time dedicated to helping people with their health. I also wrote a poem for Holly Willoughby. I think she is a stunningly pretty lady. One day we were doing a feature on hair removal on the legs. As a joke I went to a shop and bought a fake beard. I was going to attach it to my leg and whip my dressing gown back revealing a monster ball of black hair. I imagined Philip reeling back, then laughing when he realised I was playing but I bottled it in case I got told off.

I took part in The People's Book of Records depicting the longest dramatic stage death. Three other contenders were taking part. There was a line of dirty old mattresses' lining the tunnel where we were filming. Bits of old furniture were strewn about for effect.

With the cameras rolling, I started walking down an alley towards a tunnel. A man ran towards me, pretending to hurt me badly. I screamed melodramatically, scurrying towards a wall where I leant against it, gained momentum and rolled onto a dirty mattress. With blood curdling noises, I groaned and moaned so it echoed in the short dingy tunnel. Getting up, I staggered further down, knocking over a decrepit cupboard then lying on top of it.

Whimpering that I was dying, I again set off to prop myself up alongside the tunnel wall.

The cameras kept rolling. Twenty five minutes later, and after numerous cries for help I was still just about alive but running out of steam. I stunk too from lurching onto grim cushions which seemed as if they'd been used for about thirty years. I had no idea how many minutes the other challengers had taken to die and finally I spluttered my last breath and conked out.

'Has she gone?'

The cameraman filmed into my dead face.

'Yeah, she's gone.'

Running into the building where the other contestants were, I asked how long they had managed to die for. Sadly I had lost by about two minutes.

Another woman who took part managed to die for about thirty two minutes and I managed thirty. Mulling over the experience, I decided that it had been such brilliant fun to do. It can be seen on You Tube.

I watched it several years later and thought, 'I am flipping mad'.

Another call came in from another agency. 'Can you make the weekend after next to work on Midsommer Murders?'

I agreed. I'd been told it was being filmed in a stately home in Berkshire. I was thrilled. It sounded wonderful. I imagined myself in a beautiful long flowing period dress with fine jewellery sparkling for the cameras.

I left at 4am to get on set early and get some breakfast before we started filming. There was hustle and bustle as everyone lined up for their food and a hot cup of tea. A cold breeze took the edge off my anticipation.

'Alana,' a long haired lady called. She asked me to follow her. After trekking down a muddy lane we finally reached a wooden hut. On entering, I saw that there were mirrors all over the place with dressing tables.

After being sat in a chair I stared at my reflection and I could see others having their hair and makeup done. Picking up a comb, the makeup artist started to back comb my hair so that it looked like a birds nest.

I didn't want to say anything as it certainly didn't look like a slinky hairdo. An image in front of me was emerging.

Had I been pulled through a bush backwards? Roughing the hair into a frenzied ball, she sprayed hairspray all over it. She asked me to open my mouth and show her my teeth. I launched into a wide Grommet smile and she proceeded to blacken some of my teeth out.

I started to laugh but was worried that she might get angry about my reaction to her handy work on my teeth.

'What are you laughing at? 'She demanded

'On my way here, I assumed that because I was going to a stately home I was going to be some sort of lady. What on earth am I going to be?'

'Oh you're a street urchin.'

'Great', I thought, a bloody street urchin.

And it got worse. My feet and legs were laden with muslin sacks and another bag was put over my head and tied round the waist like a dress.

Today on MidSommer Murders they were portraying the French revolution, undertaking a scene of a beheading.

My role was to sit on a long wooden bench shouting at the top of my voice, 'Chop his head off.'

I was covered in chickens sitting and shitting on me, rats running round my feet, horses neighing and one bonus; a massive Labradoodle dog by my side.

In all fairness, despite my initial disappointment, I had had the most fantastic day ever. It was superb fun.

Spending all day lolling around playing silly buggers was right up my street, but when it was released on TV it was wonderfully depicted and very slick. I still giggle at my costume and how much my lady dreams were shattered.

The crew on Midsommer are so creative and very kind. The director and crew are always incredibly respectful of everyone while filming. There is no hierarchy like on some shoots. I have appeared on Midsommer Murders about six times now and I absolutely love it. It's like a big family.

Once I stood next to John Nettles and he was in a world of his own singing opera to himself. Andrea at 'Andrea Casting' runs the agency for actors and supporting artistes is a wonderful lady too. She is so pretty, vivacious, kind and she has been supportive of me in troubled times.

I could fill another book with stories of all the programmes I have been cast for. Some of my other favourites were, 'Strike it Lucky' with Michael Barrymore, 'Ready Steady Cook' with Ainsley Harriet, singing into a whisk as a makeshift microphone. I belted out, 'Zipadee do dah', 'Holby City', 'Panorama', 'Bullseye' and so many more.

Applying to go on light hearted game shows has been a hobby of mine and I hope to go on 'The Chase' with Bradley Walsh.

He is hysterical and one week, settled in front of a log fire, I was watching an episode when Bradley asked a contestant a question about someone called Fanny Chmellor and he just lost it. He giggled so much I reckon he could have peed his pants. I was rolling up on the sofa with tears streaming down my face and the more he laughed so did I. It was such a good laugh.

I've won a few prizes too on game shows: a weekend in Madrid, flying lessons, a dishwasher, £100 and a week in Spain. Unfortunately I wasn't really earning very much as a supporting artiste so Alex wasn't too happy that at the end of the year I had only made about £5,000.

I had an offer to do a commercial paying £5,000 for two weeks' work. Unfortunately I had to travel to South Africa and he wasn't keen on me accepting the trip for safety reasons. To be fair, I also had my reservations but my agent wasn't happy when I turned the work down.

TAKE A CHILL PILL

Today we awoke at Eastbourne Marina with the sun shining but am I shining? No, I am shit scared about attempting the sail back. I could have so bottled it and said I wasn't going but I knew we wouldn't get the boat back unless I sailed with Alex. She wasn't easy to handle on your own.

We needed to get some essentials before we set off to go, so we went to Asda. Our basket was full of wine, beer, cheese, chocolate and delicious sandwiches.

Standing at the checkout packing the groceries away, I handed some cash to the checkout woman and she gave me a receipt.

'Err excuse me. You haven't bothered giving me my club card points,' I complained bitterly.

Eyebrows flexed as she glanced over her glasses.

'This is Asda dear, not Tesco.'

Tucking my receipt in my bag I made a hasty retreat, apologising as I went.

'Bit of a silly moo there wasn't I?' I said, turning my head to look at Alex.

Preferring to ignore my misdemeanour, he slipped his hand into mine. I realised I was tetchy. I had the overwhelming sense to say I didn't want to sail back as I was too frightened. I believed that if I did he would go crazy at me and then there would be tears and tantrums on both sides. I determined my best option was to stay silent.

Although the supermarket had not been far, we'd taken the car, knowing we were buying lots of heavy bottles of booze. Alex screeched around the bend.

'Bloody hell, he's mad,' I cringed.

'You're driving very fast Alex,' I slated.

'Stick with me baby,' he smirked.

'If I stick with you, I'll have no hair left and poo in my knickers.'

He calmed down and we both had a giggle.

As we unloaded the car boot into a trolley, time was getting along so quickening our pace it wasn't long before we were unpacking the shopping into the boat.

'I'll do the engine and radio checks Alex. Do you want to sort the sails out?'

Creeping into the engine compartment, I confirmed that the oil was fine and the marine filter was clear of weed. There were no visible signs of any leaks, plenty of water in the coolant, the fan belt was looking good and the engine check was completed apart from the exhaust.

Up on deck I helped with putting out the winch handles. I tested the fog horn right behind Alex's head, pinched his bum, giggled and took off the navigation covers. Unlocking all the compartments, I observed that the eight man life raft was in the correct place and fiddled with the life-buoys to make sure they were easily accessible. I had a bad feeling about today, mainly because yesterday I had seriously felt my life was in danger.

I kept my eye on the flags at the top of other moored yachts. The wind varied but had not unduly concerned me at this stage.

'Eastbourne Marina, Eastbourne Marina, Serendipity, Serendipity, Over.'

'Serendipity, Eastbourne Marina. Go ahead.'

'Good morning. We require a lock out please?'

'No problem. Make your way and when the light is green enter. Over.'

'Thank you, Serendipity out.'

Squeezed into the lock with several other boats, the skippers and crews appeared to be in good spirits. A boat full of burly men all wearing the same T shirts cracked jokes, lifting beers to their lips. I considered it was a stag do. One chap cuffed another around the head, and then smacked him in his paunch. If they weren't careful one of them might find himself in the drink.

Being that rowdy now, I dreaded to think what mayhem would ensue later on. When we were in Yarmouth one evening, a group of middle aged men, all drunk, were hollering, shouting and trying to climb up onto the wall from their boat. I couldn't figure out why.

One man did the splits and fell into the water. They were all tugging his clothes trying to get him back on the boat. I stood watching for ages, as you do. Eventually they got him on board. He had cut his head and violently rubbed his crotch but they still headed out to sea. It was a recipe for a disaster.

With the waters rising, the lock at Eastbourne eventually filled up. People were pushing their boats away from each other as the water pressure surged us forwards. Gradually the lock gates opened and we motored out to the bay. I begged the sea to stay calm. It presented well.

Contemplating Beachy Head in the distance, I decided that it looked acceptable at this stage. Motoring past the wreck on the port side and on to the safe water mark, I sighed in relief.

Out of harm's way, we hoisted the sails. Within minutes we were making six knots through the water. I imagined being on the shore and staring out to sea. Serendipity must appear so beautiful, gracing the water, elegant and showy at the same time. I knew sailing had become my passion in an odd sort of way. We had a love hate relationship at times.

What a woman Dame Ellen MacArthur is! Fearless, inspirational, a massive competitive sailor and so tiny in stature!

Fortunately I heard on the radio that she had organised a talk at a local hotel in Brighton and I didn't need to be told twice. I booked a ticket, arrived early and took a front row seat.

She is a complete natural sailor, unlike me who sees fear in everything I do. Amazingly she raced single-handedly non-stop around the world in the Vendee Globe in 2001, just a spring chicken at twenty four years old.

Living at sea for up to ninety four days, she discovered that victualing properly for the boat meant success or failure. She learnt that resources, such as material, food and energy, are paramount to keeping going. Inspiring her to look at the waste in the world and encouraging us to only use what we need, she proudly announced that she only uses one sheet in the toilet, preserving the trees and loo rolls of the world and ultimately, saving the planet from death and destruction.

I couldn't get over how tiny she was - maybe, a size 8 or 10. I tried to visualise her at sea on her own. I knew I couldn't go that far with sailing. I was in awe of her that evening and left the hotel feeling more determined to carry on sailing, even if I did find it purgatory at times.

She is a tiny female who packs a big punch. With her campaign to save the planet, Ellen is a true wonder that I admire so much.

In about an hour we would approach Beachy Head, east of the Seven Sisters. Astonishingly, the cliff there is the highest chalk sea cliff in Britain and it rises to 530ft above sea level. So it is no wonder that hours after we sail past the cliff we can sight it.

On very clear days, standing on the peak of the cliff you can actually see to Dungeness in Kent to the east and Selsey Bill to the West. Chillingly though, it is a notorious spot for people to commit suicide and it is reported that up to twenty people leap from the cliff to their death each year. I suppose the fact they have instigated a Beachy Head Chaplaincy team who patrol to stop potential jumpers is a step in the right direction. They also have signs for the Samaritans with their telephone number, urging people to call for help rather than take that leap.

As we neared Beachy Head I prayed the wind to stay steady. Yesterday really had taken its toll and I was so tense with stress that my head and body hurt.

We sighted the light house with its red and white striped tower standing under the cliff.

Since 2011 they had said that they can no longer afford for the light house to be painted, so they were going to leave it to return to its natural granite grey which would be difficult to see on misty days. Thankfully, this week, I heard on the radio it had finally been painted again.

I found it fascinating to find out that the light house was built with a temporary cable car transporting workers to work out on an iron platform into the sea. I had always hoped they would find the funds to paint her again.

This navigation tower came into use in October 1902. Three keepers monitored the light-house and maintained its function until 1983 when it became fully automated and the workers were withdrawn from their duties.

I stared at the waves ahead. Thank God it seemed calm enough, apart from about 100 feet ahead where I could see birds diving into the water in frenzy, like darts hitting a board.

It seemed unusual behaviour, a performance I had not seen before. I commented to Alex that I felt something was happening up front.

'Dolphin,' Alex bellowed, 'over there!'

He pointed to the starboard side of the boat just ahead. I leapt over to the side and leant wide out, craning my neck to see them but the sea bore no sighting for me. Ten minutes later I gave up.

Sitting back in the cockpit I was moaning bitterly that he had seen them and I had not.

'It's not fair. You know how much I love dolphins. Why won't they show themselves? Are you sure you saw them?' Alex came over and gave me a peck on the lips.

'They might come back sweetheart, keep looking.'

By the time we had steered to the turning point just off Beachy Head it was time to tack. I leant over the winch with the handle and out of the corner of my eye I spotted a dolphin to the port side.

'Yes, dolphins!' I screamed in excitement.

Adrenaline surged through my body, my heart pounding and my eyes shining with delight at these beautiful cetaceans.

'Turn the music up Alex. They like the music.'

Alex hammered down to the CD player, cranking up the Caribbean music. Leaning over the safety rail as far as I could, I reached out my hand waving it frantically, hoping they would come over to me.

Their streamlined bodies coursing through the water at speed enabled their dorsal fins to leave a wake behind them. Shooting into the distance, they turned and were once again flying through the water towards us.

Their beautiful curved mouths projected a warm feeling like they were smiling at me and as they swum passed, they blew misty water sprays from their blowholes.

I felt so blessed after seeing them at Selsey Bill. Again we were being treated to another thrilling spectacle and I loved every minute of it. I can't describe the emotions I was experiencing. Such intense excitement was possibly a sign to me of their protection.

It was a bizarre moment in my life when I felt the dolphins had sensed the fear instilled in me from yesterday. They had come to support me, to let me know today's sailing would be fine.

It was uncanny that they had returned to another place where I had felt very vulnerable. It was a realisation that left me sensing that they really are one of Earth's most intelligent mammals. After enhancing the journey for a few minutes, I felt deflated when they swam away. I continued to scan the sea for a considerable while afterwards, trying to find them again but for now it really was time to tack back towards Brighton. They had gone.

I texted all the family, relaying the events of our second dolphin encounter and mentioned the fact that I thought they had been present to reassure me.

I expect my brothers thought, 'Silly cow'.

Families are a funny phenomenon. Kacie is a great mum; she doesn't always get it right but do any of us? School doesn't give us lessons in motherhood.

One year we were on holiday when our boys were in their late teens and, as it transpired, girl mad. Bustling along the hotel grounds they were off to the night club which wasn't due to end until about 2am.

I was sound asleep when I heard a faint knocking at my door which woke me up. Opening the door revealed Kacie in her dressing gown.

'You OK?' I enquired, a bit concerned.

Whispering she replied, 'Yes, I'm OK but the boys have come back and they have loads of girls in their room. Do you think they are alright?'

'Yes Kacie, of course they're alright. Go back to bed.'

'No I want you to come with me,' she beckoned.

'What on earth for? I yawned.

'I just want to go down there, please,' she begged.

So I grabbed a warm dressing gown, some slippers and off we set along the corridor.

On reaching their room we could hear giggling. Kacie put her ear to the door.

216

'They are fine Kacie. Come on, let's go back to bed you silly moo.'

Instantly she reached into her dressing gown pocket and proceeded to stuff what looked like condoms under the door.

'Oh Kacie, what are you doing?' I questioned.

On the other side of the door you could hear the voices go quiet. It went completely silent then I heard her oldest son say, 'What's that noise?'

Then my son said, 'Someone's poking something under the door.'

Footsteps ensued and then reams of laughter.

'Oh shit! Condoms!' her son shouted.

Immediately the door flew open.

'Mum, what the hell do you think you are doing?'

He was genuinely very cross.

Picking them up, he threw them at her and within seconds the girls who were in their room left in a hurry.

Her son was livid.

'What on earth are you doing mum? Go away. Look what you've done now.'

Awkwardly Kacie retreated and soon their door slammed shut. Kacie was given several evil eyes for the rest of the week and the lads had seriously suffered at her hands on this occasion. Those girls permanently steered clear of them.

Every now and then it might be daughters who embarrass you like I did with my mum. My husband had worked for a company many years ago and they were running a short story competition but employees or partners were not allowed to enter.

I decided to take part but put my mum down as the author and omitted to tell her that's what I'd done. Several months later my mother had a phone call from the local press saying that her story had been selected as a runner

217

up in the competition and the paper wanted to interview her.

She phoned me up to tell me about this weird call she'd received and when I unashamedly told her what I'd done she was none too pleased. The following week she endured a local reporter picking her brains on her inspiration for the story and how had she managed to produce such a romantic quirky piece. She was asked to smile for the clicking camera.

I was as proud as punch. There was a big photo feature and write up praising her achievement displayed on the front of the local paper.

Mum made it quite clear it was not at all funny and she had not been happy about telling porky pies, I found it funny. Bless her. Mum's easily embarrassed.

A separate incident in the supermarket left her speechless. It was Christmas Eve and I had lots of people coming to dinner for Christmas Day. Marching around the shop pushing my trolley, mum and I approached the vegetable aisle. The vegetable baskets before me were bare. There was not one potato in sight. Walking the length of the passageway, I could see that most of the veg was scarce.

How on earth could I feed twelve people on Christmas Day with no roast potatoes? Further up the aisle I could see a person's trolley with a massive bag of potatoes laying in it. A very prim and properly dressed lady pushed the trolley and, as I passed her I smiled, she gave me a dirty glance as if I was something off her shoe.

I lay in wait. She overtook. Following her close behind and stopping when she stopped, I pretended to engross myself in the few products left adorning the shelves. I suspected that a private detective would feel like this, as I closely monitored her whereabouts.

Mum was unaware of my intentions. I hovered in the background. Out of the blue it was time to make my move as the woman left her trolley unattended. Bolting down the rest of the aisle, I abandoned my mum and our own trolley. I dashed very quickly, launching, my arms outstretched, frantically grabbing her potatoes. Holding the potatoes tightly to my chest, not letting go, I ran swiftly back until I plonked them into my trolley.

My mother stood open mouthed.

'What the...'

'Shush mother. They're mine now. Quick let's get to the checkout and pay for them.'

Making a hurried departure I went to buy the potatoes.

'How can you do that Alana? That's a terrible thing to do,' she scolded.

Sidling up to me to hide, she was mortified and particularly ashamed to be stood with me after I'd helped myself to someone else's potatoes.

'She'll get over it. Anyway, she deserves it for regarding me as some piece of poo on her foot.'

I felt satisfied that I'd got my own back; anyway I had paid for them.

Next day, roast potatoes were in abundance and I didn't feel guilty one bit. But I have to confess all these years later, it hadn't been my most proud moment and I wouldn't do it now.

We were routing round a couple of fishing trawlers. Seagulls flew in flocks, swooping graciously, creating arches in the sky.

'They'd better not come over here and shit on my boat,' Alex moaned.

'Stop being so miserable! They're a marvel. I know they're a bit like scavengers at times but their feathers, their vibrancy and their curiosity is startling when you think about it.'

Thus, I encouraged him to see their beauty.

'Scavengers yes, a bit like you,' Alex directed, and then chuckled.

'I can't hear the bad jokes through my rain hood,' I retorted, holding up the palm of my hand towards him. 'I love the parrots at the animal rescue centre. They are so clever. One calls me sweetheart. Volunteering there is the only time I get wolf whistles anymore.'

'Women love me. I get wolf whistles all the time.'

He held both hands high into the air, claiming triumph.

'Shut up you silly devil. I'm surprised you can get through ordinary doors, your head is so big.'

The sail back had been uneventful with regard to safety, and the winds had been a steady force four.

'You can reverse the boat in today Alana.'

Alex wasn't encouraging me but telling me that's what I was going to do even if I didn't want to. He could see by the look on my face that I was not keen.

'You have to do it sometime. If you listen to me and do what I say, you will be fine.'

I went from relaxed to being nervous in seconds. I didn't want to humiliate myself.

'I'm not going to reverse it into our mooring Alex. I'll have a go at reversing but by the visitor's pontoons only.'

Stowing the sails away as we entered the Marina, Alex was still harping on about me reversing the boat.

I could sense conflict in the air as I took the wheel.

'Right, now give it some throttle and when I tell you to ease off, do so,' he persisted.

I peered behind me just before giving it some juice on high revs.

'OK.'

I accelerated hard but the wheel seemed to have a life of its own. It had wanted to snatch out of my hand.

'Oh Alex, it's pulling out of my hand.'

I struggled.

'Keep hold of it tight and show it whose boss. Wait for it to start turning, come off the power and then guide her round. Do it.'

'It's not turning. I can't do it.'

I raised my hands off the wheel and it swung in the direction it wanted to go.

Alex ran over and took the wheel.

'For God's sake Alana. Why the bloody hell don't you just do what you're told?' he roared.

I burst into tears.

I sat in a heap on the back of the boat, once again feeling like a failure despite the fact I had tried so hard.

Inside I had an overpowering urge to run off. That scared me. My whole being of emotions surged as if I was possessed by an evil influence. I wanted to flee, I felt very cross, I wanted to lash out. My sons could vouch for my soft, kind encouraging temperament, I felt odd.

His annoying behaviour had a negative effect on me that lasted the rest of the evening. I pulled the duvet up over my shoulders and huddled up for comfort. I wished he would be more reassuring, instead of just getting angry with me. I needed a calmer approach.

Sailing was like a tug of war for me. Tug one way and I made progress, pull another and I take a giant step back.

I could recognise the pattern I was living in. I needed to progress. I had to break the cycle, but how?

I trawled the web for help and did a search on Google about how to get over your fear of sailing.

One comment really annoyed me: 'A lot of gung-ho skippers never train their wives up to this level.'

Does he think his wife is a dog?

Another man doesn't understand why his wife refuses to put up with the stress anymore. Sailing in unprotected waters, she's fed up with sleepless nights anchored at sea in a force 8, approaching new islands and watching the depth reader, wondering if they are going to hit something. Sailing in the fog and not being able to see ahead, sailing 12 hours a day, vomiting over the side in rough weather.

Does he have an ounce of compassion or thought other than for himself?

Apparently, women have a nurturing personality. We are born to protect ourselves and our children but the husbands are the hunters.

'Why don't you see the doctor and get some anti-depressants Alana?' Kacie advised.

'Why doesn't Alex go to the doctor and ask for a calming down pill, a tablet to make him more caring and considerate. I don't need an anti-depressant Kacie. I need a husband who can show he cares,' I moaned.

Why do all these people have a perception that it's the woman's fault? Maybe the men put them under such a strain! Why that poor woman would complain about being at anchor for three days in a force 8 is beyond me! What did he want? Sex every ten minutes, a blow job every hour, grapes fed to him and a fan of feathers cooling him down? Oh, don't forget a cold beer too!

Stupid idiot! He should take personal responsibility for his actions too. Maybe a weather forecast or two might help him and also stopping in sheltered waters or in a marina might be sensible.

A website asks, 'What are you frightened of?' Ask yourself this question. You might find the answer to your problems. This is a good place to start.

Thinking hard, I start to appreciate the progress I have made and the passages I had completed, despite at times thinking I am going to die.

That's it, 'die'.

I was frightened of dying at sea.

I didn't though, did I? I am still here. I didn't die.

The walls of waves buffeted our boat but I didn't die. I helmed the boat in a force eight and I didn't die. I've reversed the boat and I didn't die. Now I contemplate that I have achieved all of those things and I just didn't die. I am still here to tell the tale.

What other times in my life have I felt fear? What did I do to help myself?

Standing in an aircraft hangar five years ago as a participant in a fear of flying programme, I'd been selected to take part due to a very embarrassing situation on an airplane coming back from a holiday in Greece.

I'd taken two diazepam tablets on the flight back to calm me down but the drugs hadn't worked. Squeezing this poor strangers hand for support, I unwillingly let go of his clasp as I made my way to the toilet in the middle of the plane. Pulling my knickers down to my ankles, I gingerly squatted over the bowl, my bum waving in the air as the turbulence hit.

Holding on tight to the sink at the side of me, I tried to direct the stream where it belonged. I gritted my teeth, maintaining my grip as the craft bumped violently up and down. "Bing! Bing!" A very unpleasant urgent sound rang in my ears and a red sign flashed, indicating that I should go back to my seat.

Flustered and in a blind panic, I did just that. I opened the door, barged forward and shuffled out with my thong pants still round my ankles.

A red faced stewardess grabbed my arm.

'What's wrong?' she blathered at me.

My immediate thought was, if she doesn't know what's wrong and she's asking me what's wrong, then it's definitely time to panic.

'I don't know what's wrong. Why are you asking me?'

I burst into tears as she tried pulling up my knickers for me.

Bending down and huffing, she reassured me there was no problem other than that the captain had requested people to take a seat as there was some turbulence predicted ahead.

I held my head low, not even wanting to walk along the aisle.

Staring passengers reacted variously to my outburst. Quite a lot were laughing at me and a couple verbalised their pity as she led me soothingly back to my seat.

Once again the elderly man had the life crushed out of his supporting hand. I bet relief washed over him when we finally landed. It was peculiar to gain such help from a stranger. He had offered me his hand and I took it, hardly letting it go for four hours.

In the aircraft hangar I learnt that if you have a fear, such as my hatred for spiders, it's essential to face it with humour. Apparently you have to imagine the spider is big and hairy but with a smile as a big as a banana. He has to have a comical face with big clown eyes and a funny hat on his head. When he walks he is drunk and falls over. Give him a stride like John Cleese. Make him really funny, so he brings a smile to your face.

'Did you know that you are more likely to be kicked to death by a donkey on your doorstep than die in a plane crash?'

'Wow that made an impact.' I called out to the trainer on the course.

'Imagine the plane is like a fish going through the water. A fish doesn't get a smooth ride. Occasionally the water roughens a bit and they will go with the flow. An aeroplane is the same. It's travelling through air. Sometimes there are air pockets and the plane drops but it can't go too far down. Imagine a roller coaster you are having fun on. Don't think negative thoughts.'

He walked back and forth along the line of us forty frightened flyers. Taking part in workshops all afternoon had been truly inspiring.

'Train your brain to use visualisation to your advantage. Desensitisation techniques will help and exposure treatment too and later today we are going on a flight.'

I suppose there was some truth in the success of visualisation as I recall practicing for an interview. I had taped a row of monkey faces to my wall and practiced my presentation to these pictures to get it word perfect. It helped.

My mother's advice was to imagine the panellists in the nude. Superficially this was supposed to make me more comfortable but imagining people's bits and pieces was far from my mind when I finally delivered my lecture.

When I boarded the plane that afternoon, I sat on my own. Accelerating down the runway, I had no hand to hold. I kept my knickers firmly up and remained cool. I couldn't believe it. I was fine.

So how could I apply this to my sailing fears?

What's my problem? Instantaneously it was like a light going on. My problem was confidence.

It was unlikely I would die and I was worrying what other people would think of me.

My first plan was to tackle the reversing of Serendipity. It was something I had to master. But having Alex as my trainer was not an option!

I looked at my watch. Plenty of time!

I grabbed my coat and jumped in the car. Speeding towards the marina I knew time was running out.

Ancasta would be closed in an hour and I needed to see Bob. Coat flowing, I ran from the multi storey car park through the hustle and bustle of the crowds. Sitting at his desk as I burst through the door, Bob flashed a cheery smile.

'Hi Bob. Do you know anyone you could recommend, a Yacht Master who would be happy to help me learn to reverse our boat? They can have a free sail on the boat as payment?' I babbled, smoothing my dishevelled hair down.

'Are you having problems then?'

'I just can't reverse her in. She's so different to Water Baby; I find it a lot more difficult. There's such a pull on the wheel and I struggle to control it. Alex starts shouting at me and then I turn into a big mess,' I pleaded.

'Look, why don't I help you. I'll do it.'

Bob's kind face stared at me full on.

'Oh would you do that? I'd appreciate it so much. I'll do my best but promise you won't shout at me.'

I gazed to the floor.

'Give me a ring when the weather improves, a day during the week when I am not working, and I'll come and help you. I definitely won't shout at you, I promise.'

'What a rock he is!' I thought and I beamed at him, thanking him over and over again, secretly wanting to give him a big hug to tell him that he was my hero.

I had to change my timid approach. I worried that I might hit another moored boat. I fretted that I could damage the hull, smack into the visitors' pontoon, look a fool. Well fool or no fool, I needed to conquer this.

I must keep a positive attitude. If I hit another boat, that's not ideal but I wouldn't do it on purpose. We can use fenders to protect them and vice versa for Serendipity.

226

I breezed out after chatting with Bob, reasoning with my situation and tackling it head on, deeming it a massive step in the right direction.

Since my failed attempt at reversing, I'd dreaded the time in the future when I'd have to do it again, but on returning from seeing Bob I was keen to tell Alex of my plan but not sure when to approach it.

Coming in from work it was clear he had been to the card shop. It was my birthday the next day. He snuck into the bedroom and I heard his bedside cabinet drawer slam. As he breezed past, I picked up a piece of paper that fell out of his pocket when he removed the card. I sneakily glanced at it. Clearly it was a receipt from a company called Rock Bottom Prices.

As he surfaced from the bedroom, I handed him the receipt.

'There's a receipt here from a company called Rock Bottom Prices. What's that for then?'

'Err, you're birthday present.'

'Oh you've pushed the boat out then? Gone the whole hog and bought something incredibly special?'

I pulled his leg, laughing. He smiled back.

'Is it a rock for my bottom?'

Again I goaded and as he entered the kitchen, I flicked some water at him. Running towards me, he scooped up a handful of liquid and chucked it back at me.

Within minutes we were giggling, laughing, scrapping at each other's clothing, trying to get water down the front of each other's tops.

Puffed out and both breathing really deeply in between shrills of laughter, we finally gave up attacking each other.

Our frosty moods disappeared.

I awoke to a beautiful bottle of Boucher on, my favourite perfume, and a cute card with two cuddling bears on the front.

Later on in the day, sitting in a restaurant in Brighton marina, I plucked up the courage to tell Alex that Bob was going to help me reverse Serendipity but I was unsure if he was happy about this. He nodded and reiterated that he could teach me, assuring me he would help me but I knew this just wouldn't work.

We could hardly understand the waiter. He was a friendly chap but neither Alex nor I could make out what he was saying. 'Bloody hell, why do they employ people who can hardly speak English, it's ridiculous I have no idea what the bloody hell he is saying.'

He believes in giving everyone a chance but this guy really did lack even the ability to answer any of our questions. Alex suddenly seemed very belligerent towards the waiter and as the waiter stood poised with his pen, Alex on purpose let out a long sentence of complete babble.

'Wah, Wah, Rumpty, Dumpty, Woo, Woo, Oogeee, Floppers.' I stared at Alex; it was really out of character for him to behave in this way. The waiter tilted his head to one side,

'You say what?' I could just make out his question.

As red as a beetroot, I butted in, 'Oh he didn't say anything; he just wasn't sure about the menu. Can you come back in five minutes please,' I turned him away. 'Alex, what the hell did you do that for?'

'Well it really annoys me, I can't understand why they would employ someone who can't understand English, let alone speak it.'

'Oh don't be mean, bless him, his mum loves him. He's someone's son Alex, don't be rotten, he's doing his best.'

Secretly we did laugh though; it's very unusual for Alex to make a fuss. Returning to the table the waiter smiled. With great difficulty he eventually took our order. When the food arrived it was all wrong. Trying to persuade Alex not to complain wasn't easy. 'Happy birthday Alana, better luck next year,' I thought to myself. Maybe he was tetchy because I had arranged help from another source.

My birthday wasn't as much fun as I thought it was going to be but I remember one Christmas, down at our local pub, the landlord had installed a talking moose's head on the wall. It came with a microphone and when you spoke the mouth activated. Opening and closing in synch with our voices, it was funny. Six of us were seated around the table right next to the warming log fire.

The moose was positioned directly to the side of my head. We named him Monty. To our left were the men's toilets. Every time a man went to the toilet I gave a running commentary as he approached the door.

'Do you have a bit of a problem with your bowels?' I growled in a very deep moose voice. At least it was how I imagined a talking moose would sound like.

'Do you have a bit of a situation going on there?'

'Lean well back.'

Everyone at the table was in hysterics and as the chaps approached they found it funny too. Scuttling back out from the loo, we would give each person a cheer on completion of their visit. Passing the microphone around the table, we all took turns in being, 'Monty.'

As a man walked towards the loo, on every step my brother made farting noises into the microphone and the moose moved it jaws in unison.

Consuming quite a few drinks, our antics kept us amused for hours. The day Monty was taken down and they refurbished the pub was a sad moment. He'd been great fun. Rest in naughtiness Monty, you were the best.

My birthday passed fairly quietly with no more erratic behaviour from Alex and in the evening I checked the weather forecast.

Over the last couple of weeks the weather during the week had been foul. Weekends had been slightly better and we'd been able to sail. On returning to the marina, there was no mention of reversing the boat, Alex just did it. Regularly I was checking the conditions at sea, hoping for a good spate of weather during the week, so Bob could help me.

Finally, I spied a weather forecast: Sunny, force 4, my eyes lit up. I called Bob.

'Hi Bob, how about Monday, Tuesday and Wednesday of next week, all systems go if you can come along?' Firm arrangements made. Time to panic!

Remember the spider Alana, I encouraged myself, treat it as a giggle. I tried to keep thinking of my friends and how I have always pushed them ahead when they have been struggling and having negative moments. My philosophy has always been never to give up.

I dragged myself out of bed and zoomed towards the awaiting demon. I happened to be very nervous.

Feeling the breeze against my skin, I could tell it was not a force 4. Perhaps it was verging on a force 3. Pleased the winds were lighter today, it would give me half a chance to get it right.

Deep down, I was seriously feeling sick. It wasn't sea sickness, but knowing I would struggle was upsetting me. I had to get over the embarrassment. I didn't want to fail. I wanted to be like Ellen MacArthur, fearless, brave, determined and clever.

'Right, we'll practice over here by the visitors pontoons, there's plenty of room here for now.' Bob reassured me, looking at my face.

'When berthing a vessel, you need to keep assessing the situation and conditions around you all the time. Ask yourself what direction is the wind coming from? Check flags around you. Is the wind strength going to impact on your manoeuvre? Is there a tidal stream to deal with? I wondered if he could see how frightened I was feeling. 'Get a feel for the wheel, reverse a little, think about what's happening and then go forward. Then try again.'

Growing the revs, I gently pulled the throttle back and reversed very slowly. I could feel the wheel pulling against me. I tried to straighten her up, so I could finally steer the boat backwards and round the end of the pontoon. I persevered trying harder each time.

'Well done, keep trying over and over again. Once you are comfortable with the way she feels, we'll try to reverse her in tighter to the pontoon.'

A crowd had gathered up on the breakwater watching my every move.

'I wish they'd stop nosing.'

Stomping along the pontoon, a heavy built man made his way towards us, 'Do you need help getting in?' he bellowed out to us.

'No thank you, were just practicing, thanks anyway.' That's exactly what I didn't want, an audience but what I wanted and what I was going to get were two completely different things. Gazing up at the row of bodies leaning over the top of the wall, their faces loomed like a load of vultures. Right think of them as a bunch of clowns, I persuaded myself, ignore them, pretend they are not there.

'Go in tighter this time, nice and gently does it.' Bob was firm but encouraging.

As I neared the pontoon I started shouting, 'Nervous, nervous, nervous.'

'Come on your doing well.'

Yes, I did it perfectly. Chuffed to bits, I smiled widely. Over and over again

I reversed her in. I'd experienced a few teething problems but finally handling her sufficiently to say my attempts had been successful.

For tomorrow Bob and I agreed I was designated to be skipper and he would be a crew member. I was to be totally in charge, he was going to be present but not in a teaching capacity. The whole day would be governed by my instructions and ultimately I would be reversing her in.

After a sleepless night, I rolled out of bed and dressed warmly. I checked the weather forecast. 'An excellent day for sailing,' I thought.

Scrambling over the boat like a rash, I completed the engine checks. Unzipping the sails, I prepared the ropes. Unlocking the locker for the life raft, I slipped the winch handles into their holder's. I paused and took a look around me. Gripping one of the wheels tightly, I raised myself on to tip toes so I could see the bow clearer; she was so long and graceful. Gently placing my feet back on the ground I engrossed myself in her beauty and the wonderful workmanship. Today was one of the most significant days in my life. I had to make this work.

I stood in awe of Serendipity, I never knew I could come this far.

DEATH AND EVIL

I recalled the first day when venturing out on Water Baby. Screaming for fear that we were going to tip over. The difficult times I'd had with Alex on my journey to sail. I had never given up no matter how hard it had become. Self-preservation is a skill I had to learn when I was a little girl.

I sat down on the seat behind the wheel in the cockpit and drifted off thinking about my childhood. Our mother had been in hospital long term. Kacie, Colin and I were frightened because we had to stay with our Grandparents. Unfortunately there had been no one else to look after us, so my mum had no choice.

Freezing cold temperatures racked my body as I rummaged through the broken toy box. I was sitting on the stone floor in their ramshackle conservatory of their bungalow. I could see my breath. I lifted each doll up and I gaped at their dirty soulless faces, their eyes gouged out. Kacie had poked them out. Each of the heads bore fine tufts of straggled nylon strands of hair, jutting out from mostly bald scalps. None of the dolls had any clothes on, their bodies discoloured from age and filth. They were never cleaned.

Ever since I could remember the toys had never changed. The ripped books were so old they fell apart in your hand. Rust had formed over most of the faulty metal toys. Generally the paint had erased itself over the years, so everything in the box was black and useless. It wasn't a toy box but a sad broken wooden chest full of trash.

I wondered why Kacie had poked the eyes out of the dolls. Trauma? Boredom? Fear? Leant against the wall behind the toy box rested Granddad's walking stick, for years it tormented me. Fear shivered through my body every time I saw the thick worn brown knobbly wooden stick. My torso bore the bruises of its beating. Hanging off of a nail in the brick wall was Granddad's leather belt with a chunky buckle.

I had been stripped bare on many occasion and thrashed with the end of the belt, until I could cry no more. Huddling into a foetus position was the best way to protect myself, had I learnt that or was it instinct? Anything he had was a weapon, shoes, slippers, poker and the cinder brush. I was aged just seven and my brother and sister eleven. I have no recollection of a happy face, or a feeling of emotional happiness, the house was full of evil.

I hear people talk about their upbringing and how in years gone by physical violence was accepted and life was tough, but his behaviour was so extreme, he behaved like a devil.

There was no reason for the beatings. My Grandfather was a psychopath (I called him the iron rod). Just a loud sigh could instigate a thrashing, so we kept silent at all times unless we were spoken to.

Walking the family dog Scampi in the drizzle with Kacie, Colin and Nan, the rod led us by the canal one day. By accident, my brother let the dog go. It speedily ran ahead and jumped splashing heavily into the canal. Colin ran after it, he struggled to get the dog out when the iron rod struck him repeatedly over the head with his walking stick. I could see him crumpling to the ground, his knees finally caved in and he collapsed onto the wet grass. Desperately covering his head with his arms, the blows rained down on his skull. Within seconds his body went limp, there was no life. I bent over his lifeless body, Kacie and I began screaming. He'd killed our brother, nothing on his body moved, I thought he was dead.

I tried to bend down towards him to see if I could help, when I was grabbed by my shoulders and thrown forcefully to the ground.

234

His vast body loomed over me, hitting me around my face several times, he left my head in agony, and I lay still clutching the sides of my head.

I watched in horror as my Grandfather's 6ft 4inch frame lifted my brother's limp body, he was trying to sit him up but his head flopped forward.

'Oh duck, what have you done?' Nan pleaded.

Kacie and I had just seen my Grandfather murder my brother. Kacie was wailing too and just as she went to run towards Colin, he let out a loud moan, Granddad pushed her back. He was alive. I thanked God, peering into the sky.

Too frightened to move I watched in my foetus position from several feet away. I ached to run to him and cuddle my brother. I remember he didn't go to school for weeks, in this day and age my Grandfather would have gone to prison. Our lives as children were shattered when we had to stay there.

We had to attend the local school, my nights and days were hell. Under the desk at school I would be kicked raw, punched in the playground and spat at every day. Returning to the house of horror, I never knew when we would be beaten by his great big evil hands, then locked up for the evening. Sitting at the dinner table there was always absolute silence, I hated hearing and seeing his large jaw grinding with every chew on his food. I wanted him to choke. I hated every second that he breathed around us. Wasting Nan's cooking was not an option, every morsel of what was on the plate had to be cleared. We were always forced to eat everything until we felt sick. Meal times were a complete endurance, the same as every waking minute of staying there. I can't eat desserts today, mainly as I find them repulsive from being forced to eat homemade apple pie oozing with maggots. The apples were picked from the garden and Nan never seemed to peel or cleaned them properly.

As soon as our meals were over, we were put in our rooms and the doors locked from the outside. Strict orders were given that we were only allowed to wee in the porcelain pot under the bed, anything else was forbidden.

Once in bed we were not allowed to come out of our room.

One day I was rolling around on the bed in agony. I needed to go to the toilet but I knew I would be badly beaten if I knocked on the door asking to be let out. Instead, in the pouring rain and the darkness of night, I managed to quietly climb out of the window and into the garden. It was teaming down with rain. I hid in the bushes and relieved myself frightened spiders were crawling all over me. I pitifully wiped myself clean on wet leaves. I lay in bed cold and damp willing the morning to come. I would remain awake for most of the night; on every hour, I would hear their Grandfather clock chime. In present day when I go to one of my friend's house she has a Grandfather clock with the same chime. It chills me to the bone when it dings. It takes me back to vivid terrifying memories. My life to date has been plagued by nightmares. I am being chased. I am being beaten. I am running through graveyards and evil monsters, ghosts and skeletons are attacking me. I will never have inner peace. I have no happy dreams, Alex often wakes me as I am screaming in my sleep, shaking my shoulder he rolls over and goes back to sleep. My dreams are so real they can shatter my day. Sleep does not come easily, ever!

Every day of my life I have tried to be a good mum, my son's mean the world to me. I am so proud of them and will always be there for them. I have loved and provided for them as best as I can. I have broken that cycle of abuse, which I am so proud to have done. My boys only know love, kindness and care.

There was no escape from the rod. I never blamed my mum, her health had not been good and she had to endure several operations. She says she doesn't remember her childhood, I just think what the hell must her younger years have been like? I love her to bits, she is special.

We were treated so differently from my mum's sister's children. My cousins were favoured; there were no beatings for them. When they gained their degrees at university, their pictures hung proudly on Nan and Granddad's wall.

It was clear we were the underlings. When my mother married my dad she was told she had made her bed, now she had to lie in it. I never bonded with my cousins, it wasn't their fault we were beaten and they were not. I hold no grudges as an adult but as a child I was jealous. They were treated so nicely and respected.

I asked one of my cousins if they had ever been beaten, she said, 'No.'

To this day I have no idea why we were thrashed so badly and my questions will never be answered for my Grandparents are now both dead. When I took the call to hear my Grandfather had died, I replaced the phone receiver and thought, the world is a better place.

The last time my Grandfather hit me I was fifteen years old. I was standing in the kitchen of our old house, he was visiting.

I was making a cup of tea and the kettle had been previously boiled.

'Are you making us tea?' he growled at me.

'No, the kettle was very hot, so I thought you lot had already had a cup of tea.'

'You lot, you lot, who do you think you are talking to saying you lot?' Within seconds his very large stubby hand swiped me hard from the left hand side of my face. My head swung like a scene from the Exorcist. I grabbed my face and I looked at him deep into his eyes, as I backed away. I found my voice.

'You nasty, horrible man, you are a complete disgrace for a Grandfather. You should be ashamed of yourself. I'll tell you now, you seem to think you can bash the hell out of me but I am one thing you will never control. I am going to become an adult, a mother in my own right. I will love my children, I will be successful, I will never give up no matter what you do to me, do you hear, I will never give up,' and then I ran away.

Bob broke my thoughts as he boarded Serendipity, 'Aye, Aye Skipper, let's go,' he beamed.

Now you probably think this is the end?

Five months later during this summer holiday, I had sailed for three long days in the fog; we lost our position on the GPS. Looking around we had no idea where we were. Sinister jutting rocks and cardinals loomed up from the mist. I am hanging over the canopy sounding out the fog horn every two minutes.

It's scary. My heart is beating fast, and I am stressed. This is not my idea of a pleasant relaxing summer holiday. On the fourth day, I explained to Alex that I didn't want to sail in the fog again. My plan was to get the bus to the next harbour. Alex's cousin who sails was also on board with us and said he was happy to continue sailing with Alex.

Alex became angry with me and threatened to sell the boat. So you see my challenge and quest goes on. Now it's sailing in the fog!

So ask yourself, 'Do you want to buy a boat?'

If the answer is, 'Yes!' My advice is not to run around the boat without shoes on, regardless of the weather.

Don't sit on the edge of the boat when coming into the mooring and keep a look out for neighbouring anchors.

Avoid false nails.

Don't lob sausages with an ice cream in your hand.

Do learn about the wonderful work the coastguard do, you will be amazed.

Don't be a complete numpty like me and think sailing is about drinking champagne.

Don't lift your legs up in the air to any man; they may not be a real doctor.

Do try to live life like each day is your last because one day you will be right.

Don't ever let another human destroy you, just keep proving them wrong in everything you choose to do.

****

Today is my birthday and Alex has bought me a Labrador puppy, I've named him Captain. At 11 weeks old it's his journey now. I am taking him to the boat today for a sail and I ask myself will he make it To Sea Or Not To Sea?

In 2008 I had a car accident that left me with terrible pain and two bulging discs in my neck. I had pneumonia at sea. I have arthritis in my arms and neck. I've had four stomach operations, four foot operations and only have half a bladder. I have severe abdominal adhesions.

Fracturing my leg and tearing my ligaments and getting crushed but after all this I still keep going. I will never give up until I take my last breath. Dawn Breslin is a life coach who helped me on GMTV. She asked me to imagine myself in a rocking chair at 80 years old. She wanted me to visualise myself at that age and think back about my life. What would I change about my existence if I could go back? Would I be happy to carry on the same path I was already on? Her words changed my view on life and I found a new zest. Get in your rocking chair.

Thank you for sharing my life, don't give up on yours, no matter how hard it gets. ☺

Please support your local animal rescue centre by either volunteering or sending a monetary donation. Kindly donate to the NSPCC, to stop child abuse and to Marie Curie Cancer Care.

Solent Coastguard

During my journey to write this book, I contacted the Solent Coastguard, to ask if I could visit them. I wanted to learn more about their service. Due to my lack of knowledge, I envisaged one man or woman sat in front of a computer and a radio. How naive I was. On entering, there were four Coastguards, (two men and two women) monitoring their screens and wearing headsets. On one wall was a large geographical map, outlining the area they cover. Another large map had small picture squares, which visually showed each emergency resource available to them in any given area. A large screen projected AIS and behind the desk where I sat, was a large map laid out for manually plotting the exact position of a vessel or persons in trouble.

The gentleman, who was my host, was Watch Officer Alan Waters. I was amazed at the complexity of the whole organisation and blown away when Alan told me how he coordinates a rescue at sea. This can be done either manually or by computer. A computer gets quicker results. When a call comes in and there is a new incident, the details of this are logged. Each incident has a code which will bring up specific questions which are related to the problem identified. Geographical maps and marine charts are used for observation and Alan expresses that intense training gives them local knowledge too. So if a caller describes where they are, the Coastguards hope to recognise their location. All positions are plotted on their paper Charts.

Alan created a scenario that a life raft is drifting at sea; it may have up to four persons on board. It was last reported at a certain position. He then proceeded to show me how, using the latest technology, he could assess and calculate the effect of the tide and wind on the inflatable. This would enable him to map out where they were and the radius that the rescue services needed to search. Unbelievably Alan also explained it was his team's duty and responsibility, to alert, task and co-ordinate the resources available to the Coastguard, such as the helicopter and lifeboat, where and how to search. The information he relayed to the helicopter team would be a complex search pattern, including the height and speed they needed to be at to complete the identified search area. I just assumed Alan would tell the helicopter the last known position and the helicopter would decide where to go. This is not the case. I was mesmerised.

During my time at the Solent Coastguard base all of them worked very hard. I asked lots of questions some which probably seemed a bit odd. I wanted to know, what they would do if a tsunami was known to be approaching the UK. Alan said they would give out radio warnings and deal closely with the environment agencies and local councils. Their job would be to start helping people whose lives were at risk due to flood waters. I asked about a dead whale I had seen, floating in the water and whose responsibility was it to recover it? Alan said the British Marine Life Rescue and Natural History Museum would be interested and would carry out a post mortem to see why it had died. Sometimes they disappear into the sea naturally but can be brought in to shallow waters by big tankers on their bow. Falling off when their speed decreases.

We conversed about the fact anyone can buy a boat and be on the water within an hour and that for the leisure industry, there are no regulations for a boat at sea. From my own experience and knowledge gained, a lot of lives would be saved with standard training for sea going vessels.

During World War I, there were over 128,000 sea mines around the UK. In World War II, there were over 100,000 mines in the Thames Estuary and the North Sea. Only 15-30% of mines were recovered after World War II. Still 190,000 mines remain around the UK. Often the shells and unexploded ordnance are recovered and need exploding either out at sea or taken on land to be detonated. As a sailor around the UK, I find these figures worrying.

The Coastguard does an amazing and complex job. Alan says if you get into trouble on the coast or at sea, ring 999 and ask for the Coastguard. Please respect the sea and the Coastguard's wonderful expertise and in its work. Donate to the RNLI if you have any spare cash, these services are a wonderful resource and men and women risk their lives, to save yours. On busy days up to seven Coastguards work in the office and many men and women are standing by with pagers ready to respond to your call.

Glossary

Term	Definition
AIS	Automatic Identification System – enables vessels with AIS to be identified
Anodes	A ship component for Protecting submerged metals
Boom	Holds the bottom of the mainsail in place
Cetaceans	A sea mammal
Cill	Slab of concrete at the base of a lock
Cleat	A metal fixture for mooring
Flotilla	A group of vessels on a voyage
Furl	To bring in the sail entirely on an in-mast furling yacht
Genoa	Front, triangular sail on a yacht
Gimballed	Allows an object to swing freely under gravity
Heads	Toilets for a sea faring vessel
Hoisting	pulling a rope to raise a sail
Impeller	An engine component
In-mast Reefing	A sail which rolls up into the mast
Keel	A large weight under yachts which keep them upright
Knockdown	When a yacht is blown completely on its side
Lock	A small body of water used for raising and lowering boats.
Pontoon	A wooden structure for mooring, commonly found in harbours
Preventer	A rope tied to stop the boom swinging across the cockpit
Reefing	Reduce the amount of sail out
Regatta	Event consisting of a series of boat or yacht races.

Rollers	Large waves
Slab Reefing	A sail that is dropped and stowed on the boom
Spinnaker	Large, bulging sail attached to the bow of a yacht
Warp	Another term for rope

The Beaufort scale is mentioned throughout this book and refers to wind speeds as 'forces.' The relevant wind speeds these translate to are shown below:

Force	Description	Speed		
		km/h	mph	Knots
0	Calm	< 1	< 1	< 1
1	Light air	1–5	1–3	1–3
2	Light breeze	5–11	4–7	4–6
3	Gentle breeze	12–19	8–12	7–10
4	Moderate breeze	20–28	13–17	11–16
5	Fresh breeze	29–38	18–24	17–21
6	Strong breeze	39–49	25–30	22–27
7	High wind	50–61	31–38	28–33

A Map of key Locations

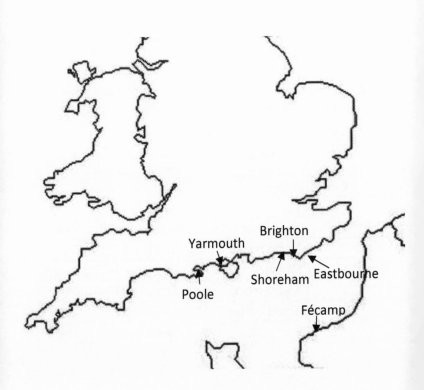

9443413R00145

Printed in Great Britain
by Amazon.co.uk, Ltd.,
Marston Gate.